I0112384

STORM YOU CAN'T WIN

GOD HAS YOUR DESTINY

Author: Willeen G. Williams

STORM YOU CAN'T WIN

GOD HAS YOUR DESTINY

STORM YOU CAN'T WIN

GOD HAS YOUR DESTINY

Author: Willeen G. Williams

THE ALPHA WORD HOUSE PUBLISHER

The Alpha Word House Publisher

Copyright ©2017 by Willeen G. Williams

Library of Congress Cataloging in- Publication Data

Washington, D.C.

Storm You Can't Win by Willeen G. Williams

ISBN- 978-0-9987241-0-2

Printed in the United States of American

STORM YOU CAN'T WIN

GOD HAS YOUR DESTINY

CONTENTS

STORM YOU CAN'T WIN

GOD HAS YOUR DESTINY

Introduction

Learn to trust God every step of the way in your life. It is imperative to trust God on any journey we be maybe facing along the way. God is worthy to be praised, and not because I deserve it no more than anyone else. God may have another plan for your life, and it is not the time for you to give up now.

I had begun to realize just on one word from God can change any situation in our life. It is essential to watch the God present all his power and Glory before our eyes just in a matter of seconds, and change can appear. We need to have the ascertain to trust God and learn to wait on his instruction to show us the right way go in life. God will teach his people how to just grab hold of faith, and trust the Lord with your life. Jesus is the rock that bigger, and taller than any human that walks on the earth today. There are all different sides, and shapes of the nature rocks on the earth that can never match up to God.   There are times you want to get on the right road, and it feels like something is always trying to hold you back in your life. Sometimes there is warfare going on in the mind, flesh, and the spirit. God had his hands on me even in my early stages in life.

The enemy will try to make you believe it was a waste of time keep calling on God. When you start seeking the face of God, and you will feel a shifting in the atmosphere the calmness will take place in your present. God is so awesome in his work, and never too late. It is to imperative keep calling on the name of Jesus every day. It is essential not never to move too fast, and make a huge mistake, and just take your time to thinks it out. God is always the head of our life, and the important step first is to acknowledge God before making any plans.

PART- ONE

_____

Call on God

One starry summer night while, I was walking, and realize in my mind that a relationship filled with love is just like a flower and it continues to blossom. One day I had looked up at the sky, and see all the beautiful work God created with his hands. The love that God has for me, and it is worthy to behold.

It is essential to understand God always be with you, and no matter what the situation a person facing in life. Love is just like a seed, plant it in the ground keep it watered, cultivate it, and the seed will grow. The love of Jesus has reached way down on the inside of you, and the love is growing every day. The Bible is a good source to communicate with God. It is imperative learned to connect with God, and it is a part of my life. It is essential to keep studying the word of God to gain knowledge and power.

The voice of God will bring you great peace in your heart, and mind. I will long to hear God's whisper in my ears, and letting me know it does not matter what time day or night you can call me. "Call unto me, and I will answer thee, and show thee great and mighty things which thou knowest not" (KJV). God wants us to look to him for the answer and do not depend on someone else to help you make the decision. The storm can't win, God has your destiny in his hands.

I had to learn to trust God every step of the way in my life. I found out along this journey asking another individual for their opinion, and it is not the right solution for my problem. The voice of God is gentle, and kind desiring to communicate the spirit on the inside of his people. When I call on God, he will come to my rescue, any day or night. I will never forget on a beautiful summer, afternoon going to lunch, and waiting for the traffic to clear

at the stop sign before pulling out on the highway. I was in

my car singing Jesus, Oh Jesus How I Like Calling Your

Name. I looked both ways, and waiting for the traffic to

pass. A big farm truck hit me while sitting in my car that

very minute, and another vehicle traveling in the opposite

directions.

Just a touch of the Master's hand

The appearances of both the trucks were traveling on the

highway. The farm truck ran off the road and hit me while

sitting in the car at the stop sign waiting for the traffic to

clear. I woke up in the hospital emergency room, and they

had to wrap me up in blankets to keep my body from going

into shock. I do not know who got me out of the car, and

long it took them to get me out. I can remember waking up

in the hospital room with blankets wrapped all over me. I

was told the blanket over me to keep my body from going

into shock. The next thing, I knew someone was placing a

neck brace on my neck in the hospital room. I was in a lot of pain, and tears were flowing down my cheeks.

I suddenly heard a voice that spoke and said I was that footstep in the sand that protected you from the death door. God said, "For he shall his give angels charge over thee, to keep thee in all thou ways" (KJV). I had started feeling a warm touch going all down the body and thanking God for his present. I knew it was God standing right by my side that day taking care of me in my storm. "I will never leave you nor forsake you, and always with you until the end" (KJV). I was thankful Jesus were right near me, and just like he promised in his word.

During this hour, I was laying on my bed of affliction and know Jesus was just one pray away to my deliverance. I had to find out from myself what pray will you do? I had experience with the Lord that very day and laying there on my sick bed, and I could feel Jesus holding me in his arm. I have learned in life there is no one like Jesus. Later, I was released from the hospital and went home to get some rest. My body was still in pain from the car wreck for weeks, and the tears were flowing down on my pillow. In the late hour of the night, I was hearing the still soft voice speaking to me, and saying it is I right here by your side. My heart rejoiced again to hear God letting me know I got you. The storm can't win, God has your destiny in his hands.

One, Tuesday morning I had decided to get someone to take me to the place where my wreck car stored. I was shocked and amazed how God brought me out that wreck. I knew there was a true, and living God that spared my life that day in the wreck. I was standing at the site just crying and kept saying Lord thank you for saving me that day. "When I think of the goodness of Jesus, and all that he did for me my soul cries out Hallelujah" (KJV). I was rejoicing in the Lord that day like never in my whole enter life. The storm can't win, God has your destiny in his hands.

God had his shield of protection all around me, and it is a blessing. God, had stopped the impact of the farm truck when it hit me from the driver side while waiting for the traffic to pass. Yes, just one touch from Jesus will make everything alright. It is a blessing God brought me out just in time and still kept me here for such an appointed season. When, I look back over my life, and begun to think things over it was nobody but Masters touch that kept me.

It is a blessing God allow us another chance to get things right. I heard the voice the Lord again "Call unto me, and I will answer thee, and shew thee great and mighty things, which thou knowest not" (KJV). Oh, the Glory of God is so awesome in all his ways, and it is beyond more than we can ask or think. There is so much power in his hands, and no one can do the things that Jesus came do for us. I believe God spoken word, and the truck came to a stop the impact and shift weight to reduce the speed. The mighty hands of

God had overturned and gave me the victory that day. Jesus can do what man think it's not possible.

Jesus "And he rose, and rebuked the wind, said unto the sea, Peace be still" (KJV). I know God has that same power right now today to control this whole universal with just a touch of his finger or speak the word. I believe everything around us is subject to the spoken voice of God, and that is awesome.

I had begun to realize just on one word from God can change any situation in my life. I had watched God present all his power and Glory before my eyes just in a matter of seconds. God is worthy to be praised, and not because I deserve it no more than anyone else. God had another plan for my life, and it was not the time for me to check out yet on the other side. The storm can't win, God has your destiny in his hands.

My plan in life was to wait a little longer to answer the call of God in my life. I was involved in an accident God spared my life, and it could have cost me everything. I was planning to live my life in another time zone, and enjoy the pleasure the of the world. "For my thoughts are not your thoughts, neither are ways my ways, saith the Lord" (KJV). I had to sit down and think about it so many times how God just still stepped into my life and took control.

If, I was still trying to sit in the driver seat and be in charge of my whole life it would have been in a total mess right today. I had learned from my mistake to move back out of the way, and let God step in my life. I had heard the voice speak a week before standing in my living room telling me to turn my life around and come now.

I knew, one part of me wanted to come, and the other part of my heart was not ready. I had to find the out the hard way sometimes in life the world will offer you material things, pleasure, and friends. There are temporary things on this earth that distract you from God. I was entangled in the world like a spider in a web trying to find a way out. A spider's lines across into many directions. I was traveling on a highway in my life there a lot of intersection many travelers along the way and did not understand the road was wide. The storm can't win, God has your destiny

Oh, when Jesus came into my hospital room and held my hand while I was laying on my sick bed. My life had changed that hour, and I began to see things in life from another perspective. It is just like looking out the wrong window trying to see the car pulled up in the yard. I had to turn in another direction to see and allow God to show me the way on this journey in life.

Jesus said, "come unto me, all that labor and heavy laden, and I will give you rest" (KJV). When I came to Jesus, my soul began to rest in the Lord with peace, and joy. I had found myself in the wilderness for many years going around in a circle and could not find my way out. I had to surrender my life unto God that very hour, and Jesus stepped in the control room.

When I came to Jesus just all wounded, broken, and the Spirit of God was beyond all my misunderstandings. There was an inner peace, and joy flowed on the inside of me. Jesus said, "Take my yoke upon you, and learn of me, for I am meek and lowly in heart, and ye shall rest unto your soul" (KJV). God had spoken, and it is already done just trust me and learn all about me to be your guide along the way in the storm. The storm can't win, God has your destiny.

We need to have the ascertain to trust God and learn to wait on his instruction to show us the right way go in life. God will let us know to just grab hold on to our faith, and trust me him with your life. The enemy will start trying to put doubt in your mind. It is imperative to let God take our life in the right direction.

The burdens on my shoulder began to shift, and the load was a lot lighter, and God done it for me. Example It was just like trying to move a sofa by myself, and I need someone to help. We can reach that journey in life, and God wants to help us and make the load lighter. When Jesus had taken the burden from me, and things in my life got better every day of my life, and the load was lighter. I was happy to see my life feel brand new. The storm can't win, God has your destiny in his hands.

Learning to communicate with God

It is imperative to learn communicate with God and spend quiet time reading, and praying before the Lord. Praying it will become an essential part of your life to talk with God, and it is exciting to be in his present. Life has an open gateway, and so many people you may encounter every day. The connection you make with God is more powerful than anything on the earth.

We know prayer is an open line of communication with you, and God. Example, we have water to drink when turning on the faucet and place a glass to catch a drink to satisfy our thirst. I had developed a hungry, and taste more of God, and just lay in his present to get a refill. My relationship with God is stronger, and I loved just calling Jesus name.

I had felt the prayer of God pull me to come back into his present, and sometimes in the midnight hour to pray. The power of God was strong in my room, and I could not disobey the voice of the Lord. It was a great experience, and God was ordering my steps in his word day by day.

I had never dreamed of my life communicating with God had a tremendous effect. The voice of God is powerful, and the sounds of the ocean tides can't match up to his Glory. It was imperative for you to read God's word, and other books, searching the scriptures along with praying. Listening is a powerful way in communication, and it is imperative to hear what steps to take next in life. We need to have a keen ear to hear the voice of God.

The lesson in the word is relating to hearing God's voice in the garden. There are seven ways to listen to communicate with God through the scriptures, and the Holy Spirit speaking to our hearts, the prophetic word (word of knowledge, word of wisdom, and personal prophecy) and Godly counseling, the peace of God, circumstances also timing, and confirm from more than one mouth. The storm can't win, God has your destiny in his hands.

These are some great indicators to listening for God's voice. "Wherefore, my beloved brethren, let every man be swift to hear, and slow to speak, and slow to wrath" (KJV). It is imperative the voice of God, and not try to move so quick on your impulse. It is imperative to understand moving too fast causes to many mistakes to occur in your life.

It is important to listen and get clearance before making any move. Example, "But the fruit which is during the garden, God has said you shall not eat from it or touch it, or you will die" (KJV). God had already spoken to Adam & Eve gave them divine instruction don't to do in the Garden of Eve. Adam & Eve refuse to follow the orders had given unto them in the garden, and it cost them to miss a great blessing from God. It is essential to always want to stay in tune with the Lord's voice and listen to the direction for your life. I must admit individuals not following God's direction, and desire to do things another way was not always the right choice it will cost you.

It is imperative to learn to stop, and listen for the clearances and proceed to go. Example, is like being at a four-road intersection, and someone has the right away to go first. It is imperative everyone does not try to go all at once, and it will cause a collision. Walking with God will come with the right direction to follow him like a road map, and listen to God. "And the peace of God will passeth all understanding, shall keep your hearts and minds through Christ Jesus" (KJV). I have learned to listen and comprehend what God is asking me to do. Listening is the first foundation to the open line of communication.

How can we communicate without first listening?   I have accepted my commandment from God and walk there in his well not my own. God's voice is the best voice anyone can every listen to on the whole earth today. I found out talking to God about certain things going on in your life, and King Jesus wants to tell nobody.

There is a total difference when talking to a man or woman, and trying share information they may tell someone else. It is imperative to stay on own one accord and listen to the divine revelations from God. You realize that distraction can cause us to lose sight on what God trying to tell you to do.

God is awesome in all his ways, and not some of the time but all the times he is good. It is important to obey the will of God, and not man desire in life to please the flesh. The devil knows when God is getting ready to bless you, and God wants to take you up to another level in the Holy Spirit. God said done, and trusting the master when the words spoken beautifully, and let you know it is all well. The storm can't win God has your destiny in his hands.

God will always want our undivided attention every day of our life. "For thy Lord thy God is a jealous God among you" (KJV). We should never put anything before God. Therefore, it is imperative to be in the face of God desiring to hear his voice, and the distractions come when your mind focused on things that are not pleasing to God. I know God is concern about us, and want you to be alert of things laying up ahead. The storm can't win, God has your destiny.

Example, Individual being jealous of another person gifts or possession will result in sin. Our heart will continue to communicate, and listen with your whole heart to the spoken words of God. God wants every part of us to worship him, and not just when things are alright in your life. You may have faced some blows unaware in your life that almost took you out at a moment notices. The storm can't win, God has your destiny in his hands.

God, will constantly warn you there is no need to fear my child, and just hearing God voice letting us know everything is going to be ok, and always trust him in the midst the storm. It is important to understand, and trust God to believe in him no matter what it look like in your life. Sometimes with the nature eye things seems to look bigger than the appearances the whole problem. It is imperative to watch God, and he makes his present know before us in the cool of the day, Sometimes God will make his appearance in the midnight hour, and everything is quite in the house.

It is an enjoy hearing God's voice in the midnight hours, and it brings a great peace to my soul. Communication is a vital source to reaching God, and in the time your needs the Lord will answer. God had created us to commune with him, and to love the marvelous things he can do for us. We should personally count it a great privilege and honor to communicate with the all Mighty King.

The connection with God is greater than silver or gold, and it can't overshadow God's nor his work on the earth. It is awesome feeling to be invited to dine with Jesus every day, and never miss a word. There been a time in your life felt things was falling apart just like wheels on a wagon rolling off a wagon, and hard to put back on. When we have right connection with God, and there is nothing too hard for God to put back in the right order in our life.

God is always concern about us all the time, and there is nothing too impossible for my God to handle. We must learn pray unto the Lord in the midst of your tears, and heart aches. Life sometimes seems like a puzzle trying to put it all together, and place things in the right order. It is imperative to communication with Jesus every day of your life.

God will hear your cry, and calling on Jesus name in the midst your storm. It is imperative to listen for a still calm voice speak to you saying. "Be still and that I am God" (KJV). It is an awesome wonder to know that God hears your cry, and understands our pain even in the midnight hour, and it does not matter morning, noon, or night.

It is a blessing to know that God is not like a man, and always there for us anytime, and hour. It is blessing just to bow down on my knees, and God right there beside you, and every step of the way. We should continue to communicate with God, and it is an important part of our life.

Connecting with God is just like taking a fresh breath of air into my body, and enjoying the blessings. I had found out that "without God" life would be impossible to manage every day. I have talked to God and found peace in every raising moment that pain, tears, and heartache try to interrupt your life. The storm can't win, God has your destiny in his hands.

We know there is no one like Jesus love that able to help us, and able to understand the ups and downs of our life. The daily communication with God helps us to cope with problems in life. The voice of God is like hearing a beautiful sound, and the flowing streams of water off the cliff of a rock.

Never forget to pray

It is essential to pray to God, and even when things are going well in your life. Sometimes along the way, things will happen, and the enemy will try to block us from praying to the Lord. It is a vital time, and we should never get too busy pray in the morning, evening, and night. Praying to God is our power of protection in the midst the storm that may try to come my way.

Prayer is just like using a hammer to drive a nail into a board, and it will penetrate right on through. I have found out through prayer, and supplication it will break down the barriers man can't move with the nature hand. The storm can't win, God has your destiny in his hands.

Prayer will change things, and it can make a bad situation turn it around for good every time. "Jesus asks his disciples a question can you watch with me for one hour" (KJV). It is important to always a watch and prays to God every day never get too busy and forget about praying. God has already commanded us to pray every day, and this his will for me to obey the word of the Lord.

"Praying always with all prayer and supplication in the Spirit and watching thereunto with all perseverance and supplication for all saints" (KJV). It is imperative to pray unto God in the Spirit to make a direct line of communication. "Devote yourself to prayer being watchful, and thankful" (KJV).

I have enjoyed spending my time with God, and ready to receive the divine words from the Master lips. Communicating with God is great, and never get to occupied in the cares, and affairs of the world it will make life a lot easier to live. It is imperative to bow and make my confession know unto God in a quiet place.

Prayer will give me the opportunity to worship, and praise the Lord for all of his goodness. Prayer is more than asking for the blessings. God wants his people to have communication, and learn about him. God wants us to make our request know to him personal, and no one else.

Jesus, will answer you when you pray

Jesus had already told us how to pray unto him every day. These are simply instruction Jesus has given us to do. Jesus disciples had an opportunity to communicate and walk with Jesus every day. It is imperative to for us to stay motivated, and in tune with God being in his presence is a great honor. Jesus taught his disciples "The Lord's Prayer, Our Father which art in heaven: Hallowed be thy name" (KJV). The same manner Jesus wants us to pray stay in fellowship, worship his holy name. It is essential to have a deep relationship with God and wait to hear his voice.

Jesus said, "But thou, when thou prayest enter into thy closet, and when thy have shut the door, pray to the Father which is in secret; and thy Father which seeth it in secret shall reward thee openly" (KJV). God is so awesome in all his ways just letting us know to come, and talk to him tell him what is going on in your life. God will listen to our needs, and direct the path to take without making any mistakes. Jesus loves us too much and desires to take care of us through all our ups and downs in life. The storm can't win, God has your destiny in his hands.

We are living in a time that prayer is vital all over the world today. Do, we have time attend sports events, and practices every day? We should always have the time to pray during the day. Jesus is important a part of life, and I enjoy being in the present of the Mighty King my Savior.

It is essential for everyone to get sincere about God, and always make it their business to put Jesus on the list first in your life. It is imperative to continue to pray every day, and it will be automatic come a custom life style for you.

It is important to stay in the face of God, and tune the things of the world out. It is imperative to stay focus with God, and seeking his face, always never get slack praying. God will always hear our cries, and it is important to listen to his voice speaking to us when we pray. Praying to God is imperative, and praying is a powerful tool in life to communicate with Jesus every day of our life.

Praying in the right place

It is imperative to meet God and communicate with him alone with no interferences. I will get in a silent place to talk to God, and listen to his voice to say here I am my child. Listening to God's voice in a peaceful spot is important to find the right result to any question. I have found myself with a lot of questions asking God and received my answers the same hour. God wants all our focus to be on him, and not distraught with the things going on around me.

How do I know when I am in the right place? It is the right place quietness, and it is just you and God alone communicating together. God wants all of us to be commit to him, and nothing else taking our attention away from the Lord. "In thy presence is fullness of joy; at thy right hand there, are pleasures for evermore" (KJV). I can feel the peace, love, and joy in the presence of God in my quiet place. It is a pleasant place to be in God, and just knowing he will comfort you in the darkest hours just before dawn.

It is imperative to understand God's voice and believe the Lord will bring you out of the storm. It is essential to find your secret closet, bathroom, pray by the bed, and close the door it is now you and God. There are times to pray for our children, and we need to spend quality time with God alone. Yes, we should always pray in the church for the sick, and over the offering and even over our food that prepared at home.

Yes, there is a total difference in praying in a congregational pray, and a secret prayer. A congregational prayer is everyone coming around in a circle, and the leader of that church prays for you. A secret pray is just you, and God alone no one know what, I am asking God to do for me. The reason a person sometimes need to be in total isolations is that God wants to speak to just you and we need to listen to his voice carefully. The storm can't win, God has your destiny in his hands.

It is imperative to close the door behind us and leave out the different kinds of distractions such as cell phone ringing, music playing, tweeting birds, dogs barking, alarm clock, television playing, family talking, and radio. It can be annoying, and it will make you lose focus on seeking God's face.

It is essential to find a relaxing place to pray, and not have to struggle with the confusion. I believe there is a possible reason Jesus wanted us to pray in secret. It is not to allow everyone to know what you are praying, and to avoid distraction. God wants all the focus and prayers offered up unto the Lord.

Praying in the right comfort zone

It is imperative to have that right kind environment to talk with God and feel the freedom. There are some couple that likes to get away and enjoy life. It is imperative to be in a quiet luxury resort to get away from the family, job, and children. It is important to reflect and delight our self in fulfilling every moment together. Couples should have time together, valuing every second that God allows in their life. The peaceful time's couples spend together it can help their relationship to grow.

Let's compare a quiet place to meet Jesus in our prayer room. I have a special place in my home, and there are scriptures on my prayer wall, and I believe every written word. God wants us to seek his face in our prayer room, and no interferences.

You will feel so relax, and comfortable in our space talking to God, and no one else can fill that block up. God is worthy of all the praise, and it is imperative to appreciate the opportunity to seek his face every day of our life. The more time you spend with the Lord, and it will allow a person to develop a stronger relationship with God. It is essential for us to stay in the Lord present to get to know God for yourself, and the path to follow. The storm can't win, God has destiny in his hands.

God timing, is not like a man and there is no clock ticking when to punch in or out of the shift. It is awesome just being able to feel the Glory of God come in the room, and a warm touch of Jesus' hand and the Lord will send an anointing to flow all over your body.

The power of God will make you feel happy and comfortable in the arms of Jesus not one can hurt you. It is imperative to be in the face of Lord, and I have experienced the peace that is extraordinary fulfill my life. There is great joy finding the right resting place in God, and there is no distraction.

PART- TWO

Traveling the wrong path

There are times in life; you may feel depressed, and you do not know which way to turn. You may experience a cold wind like it is from the outside and don't understand what is going on. Have you ever experienced that before in your life? There may have been a time in your life, and you experienced traveling a difficult path and it was a challenge because Jesus is not leading you. You may endure some sleepless nights, and you try to get out of that serious situations. It may seem like the harder you tried still no peace in your life, and you were exhausted through the storm

God will turn on a light from heaven, and to help you realize the road broad is the wrong one. The highway you on are too many travelers going in that same directions, and it is dangerous. You have thought about the confusing cycles the enemy may try to bring to stop your progress in life. Sometimes you will feel a lot of discomforts, and you are in a strange place. On your journey trying to find your way out of the storm. The storm can't win, God has your destiny.

You may have to ask yourself a question, and why you are here in this place? Sometimes we may go to a place with friends, and you thought it was ok. The road will keep getting wider, and the lights were getting dimmer along the pathway. Sometimes your heart will start pounding, and you are trying to search for the light.

Trying to get on the Right Road

It may feel like your heart were empty, and something was missing on the inside. Example, it is like going into a big empty room, and no one lives there in that place. Have you found yourself asking a question, why do I feel alone? There was no answer for you to find "at that time" only an empty spot and your heart is still yearning.

You had tried to search all over high and low still no solution. The world has so much to offer you, and it is not always good for you. The journey you had tried to find peace in the midst your storm, and your heart is filled with pain. "Jesus answered I am the way and the truth and the life" (KJV). It is like a breath of fresh air flowing through the nostril, and a great smell passing your way.

The light will begin to get brighter in your life to find peace in the midst the storm, and everything is working out for your good in life. The voice of God is like a ray of sunshine beaming in your window early in the morning. Now there is a new spark in your life, and you are ready to set sail on another journey in the beautiful sunlight in the early morning. It is a joy to see that life better now, and your heart is glazing with the joy.

Holding on to God in the middle of the storm

You are going through may be some rough spots in your life, and the storm seemed so heavy to handle. It is complicated for you to see in the midst your storm the pain, tears, disappointment sometimes bring into your life. There are different types of a storm, thunderstorm, flash flooding that may arise in the midst us on the earth.

Sometimes we can wake up in the morning and sun is shining bright, and beautiful than all sudden a storm come up from out of nowhere that evening. Life may have that same effect the first part of your day is going well, and all sudden you are facing a storm.

How do you embrace yourself through a sudden storm? I have suffered through many storms in my life some turmoil and some light tempest. "But the ship was now in the midst the sea tossed with waves: for the winds was contrary" (KJV). Jesus disciple was afraid when they were on the boat, and it is raining, windy, the board tossing at sea. The disciple was terrified and did not know what to do in the midst the storm. The storm can't win, God has your destiny in his hands.

Example, I can image a man fallen in the middle of the river, and could not swim. The individual's visibility will get unstable during this time, and they will lose their way through the storm. You can hear the voice of God in the midst your turmoil, and not knowing how long the storm lasted. Jesus went down and rescued the man from drowning in the storm. The storm can't win, God has your destiny in his hands.

Jesus had appeared to me one day in the middle of the night. Suddenly, I had heard a voice say, "be of good cheer it is I; be not afraid" (KJV). God was right there during all the hard times and my struggles. Sometimes, life will take you by a surprise, and without a warning, if we are not anchor in the Lord. A nature boat has too be anchor in case a storm come, and it will not blow away or damaged in the tempestuous in the middle of the night. Storms does not always appear during the day, and may happen at midnight.

I am not just talking about the rain, thundering, and the lighting. I am speaking about nature situation that can take place in your life the middle of the night. God will protect you through any problem that is going on in your life. Sometimes in the midst the storm pulling, shifting, tossing, and does not feel like it will ever let up.

You are still trying to find comfort ride out the storm in your life, and hoping for help to arrive soon to your rescue. I know there are different types of storms and boisterous wind that try overshadowing your life even at daybreak. I began to cry out to God please hold my hand, and don't leave me alone, and it is frightening to be in the eye of a storm. Sometimes storms will get larger, and will not move into another direction without God's permission. The storm can't win, God has your destiny in his hands.

You were crying and waiting in the midst the storm, and believing God to bring you out of the situation. There are some storms meant to stay a long time, and some storms a short awhile soon pass over. One night I was laying in my bed tears dripping on my pillow trying to find that inner peace. I was getting infuriated and down to my last count in the storm living from one day to another trying to find the right path.

Jesus had kept me on the right course in the midst the

storm, and the clouds seem to be hanging low in my life.

God had to remind me one day I am like a footstep walking

in the sand right beside you daughter. It is a blessing when

God bring you out of a storm. Sometimes it seems like it

was no ending. God, had stopped the turmoil in your life.

God has spoken, the storm is over now. The storm can't

win, God has your destiny.

Soaring above the clouds

There may be a time in your life the clouds might seem

dark, and there is no light shining. The Lord will lift you

above the storm, and place you on a solid rock. I had to

thank God for now seeing the sunshine and soar like an

eagle in the sky free, and happy to fly in the open sky. God

has delivered me from the distress, anxiety, and the thwart

in life. It is imperative to walk into your destiny and fulfill

the vision to do the well of God. I know there is a place for

God's people, and God will allow us to find a resting place to spread our wings.

Jesus said, "But they that wait upon the Lord shall renew their strength, and shall mount up with wings as eagles, and they shall run, and not be weary, and they shall walk, and not faint" (KJV). It is imperative wait on God, and the Lord will bring you out of your storm. There is a bright light peeking through the cloud, and you will see a new day up ahead. God able to catch you in the palms of his hands, and the Lord will not let you fall to the ground. "My Father, which give them me, is greater than all; and no man is able to pluck them out of the Father's hand" (KJV). God is so protected, loving, and wise to watch over us during the storms in our life.

God is awesome, and the Lord knows the turmoil, and the pressure you endure in the storm. It is amazing how "the King of King and the Lord of Lord" (KJV). God will step in on time in the middle of the storm. A female eagle knows when the babies are in danger and come to spread her wings over the nest to the protect the baby eagle. God has put his shield and protection up around me, and I am soaring my wings like an eagle in the sky. The storm can't win, God has your destiny in his hands

God will lift us up above the head of our enemy and keep you safe for his Glory. God is love, and his kindness will allow you to sail free, and above the thundering, the lighting, and rain that is in your life. My heart is overwhelmed, and to see that God is willing to love us just that much to allow you soar through the clouds, and open a silver lining that will fill us with a new life. Jesus said, "Because he had set his love upon me; therefore will I deliver him: on high, because he knows my name" (KJV). It amazing that God is all knowing, and see everything that was happening in our life.

It was Jesus love that lifted us, and there were times you felt like nothing else found would help you through the storm. God was right there to carry you, and Jesus is never too busy to come and see about us. It is essential for us never get too busy pray and forget about God.

Sometimes in life people can make a mistake get hurt, example injury their foot. There is a healing process we must first go through before walking on that foot. Jesus will lift you above that storm, and help you to soar again like an eagle in the sky. The Lord will lift you up without any fear of your past hurt. The Lord knows your appointed time to go, and free without any distraction in your path. God is the wings under your arms to ride out your storm, and carry you over the valley. The storm can't win, God has your destiny in his hands.

It will seem like an uphill battle in life and try to stay track on with God. You must remain focus on the Lord and don't try to do things yourself because God is the pilot in your life. You will totally depend on God, and stay in the direction of your destiny, and to finish your course. God will teach you how to soar above every problem that arose in your life, and to stay in tune with God. Jesus will allow us to excel in him, and seeing the works of the Lord powerful hands operating in your life. The love of God can produce life in every living creature on the earth.

God will pick you back up like mother did a little bird that felled, and the bird needed help to fly again. It is imperative to understand the same God that granted the stars to hang in the heaven. Jesus placed the moon in the sky, and allow it to rotate every day to glow give us the night. Every tear dropped we shed God can see them big or small.

"Thou tellest my wondering; put thou my tears into thy bottle: are they not in thy book" (KJV). God is concern about us, and the Lord see the tears that flow from our eyes to save them, and record it his book. God notices everything about us and understands, and it is right by our side through the ups, and down in your life. The eyes of

God are in every place, and smiling upon us, and enjoying the labeled made by his hands. God does care about everyone situations and love us.

The voice of God silent every negative doubt, fear, pain, cares of the world. God has all the power to speak the word done no matter what large or complex.   It is amazing that Jesus will wipe every tear drop away, and give you the strength to get back on course to soar above the dark clouds. God said, the victory and there is no failure in the King. "That that wait upon the Lord shall renew their strength: they shall mount up their wings as eagles; they shall run and not be weary; and they shall walk, and not faint" (KJV).

You may have been knocked off course in the midst your storm, and it was hard getting back in the right position. God want us to wait on him, and get on the correct track to rise over the dark clouds. It is better to step aside and let Jesus give us the instruction to follow and get back on course to soar over the storm. God will give the directions, and the plans are in the Master's hands. We have to learn to get out the way of God, and don't hinder things because it will take longer to overcome your victory.

"But now, O Lord thy art our father; we are thou clay, and thy our potter; and we are the works of thy hands" (KJV). God will let you know it does matter which road we thought might be right for us, and it is all in the hands of the Lord. Sometimes you will try to soar in one direction, and it was not the correct path to follow.

You may have fallen in grieve to see the dark clouds hanging low over your head. It was the hands and the Mercy of God that reached down to pick you up out of your storm. Example, sometimes even nature hard rain, we may have to pull off the highway and get clear visibility to traveling to your destination. God will allow us to go through the turmoil, and cry out to the Lord for the right direction. There is a place God wants us to be, and trust his instructions to rise over the right path, and to see clearly along the way to our journey. The storm can't win, God has your destiny in his hands.

The Power of God

Even in the darkest hour of your storm, God is right there in the midnight. There were times we may feel like God left us, and you could not trace his footsteps along the way. Jesus said, "I will never leave you nor forsake you" (KJV). God was letting you know there no need of worrying about anything he always there for you.

It is imperative for you to know Jesus, and he will always be there for us. The broad road you traveled, and you may have thought real friends were walking in the same direction. You found out they were not a true to friend, and they walked away several times when you needed them the most in your life. Even though the road got hard sometimes too hard to handle, and you faced with the never-ending disappointment that life brought your way. You asked yourself a question how do I get close to God?

One day, I found the answer been searching for a long time, and your desire to tap in the present of God. You needed to have a faithful relationship with God, and seeking his face in the midst your storm. Your mind has to be renew in Christ, and meditate on his word day and night, and to see the love, peace, miracles unfolding from the hands of God in our life.

I have found great peace and comfort in the present of God, and watching him move in an awesome way like never in my life. There have been times in my life feeling depress, and no one to turn to for my answer, and God will bring peace through prayer. Prayer is a powerful tool to use communicating with God and get your answer.

Sometimes in life things seems confusing, and after talking to God about the matter, and things will get turned around for best outcome in my situation. God, has never failed me yet, and it is imperative "Trust in the Lord with your heart not lean to my own understanding" (KJV).

It is essential for us to go pray first and you try not to workout things on our own, and make a mess. God will always be on time and is never late, nor busy when you call on the name Jesus. God will answer when you call him the first time, and is right there anytime morning, noon or night. There is power in prayer when we pray with a sincere heart, and never doubt God's word.

God will move on your behalf when your prayers are offered up to him, worship, and praise his Holy name in the Spirit and truth. Prayer is a powerful weapon to help tear down the walls of the devil that tries to stop us from getting in the face of God. I will always count it as a privilege God will allow us the opportunity to come worship in the Spirit.

There is power in prayer, and it gives me great joy to find the peace of God that very same hour.

I know when God shows up in my present something is getting ready to happen, and the situation is no longer going to remain the same that day. It is imperative we need to keep an open line of communication with God, and you can spend that unique moment to Glorify the Lord's name. The power that lays in the hands of the God will move in your life, and Jesus will stop any storm that tries to reach the surface point in your life. Prayer is a powerful weapon that can unlock any closed door in the past or the future, and it will bring forth blessings in the midst you.

There is no secret what pray can do, and God can do anything there is nothing too complicated for the Master's hands. I will just continue to pray and watch God break every chain, and move every mountain in our life. Sometimes, the situation feels like a little too much for you to bear, and when you fail down on my knees crying out to God in prayer everything will turn around in your favor.

I had to learn, and try God for myself and found out that prayer is the solution, and your faith with help unlock the door. The storm can't win, God has your destiny in his hands. It is imperative to understand that praying with an earnest heart toward God openly full of compassion, and God will answer your prayers. God want to bring you up higher, and learn to Glorify Jesus name Praying to God will bring you closer, and learning to appreciate his love for you. It is essential for you to pray, and you will believe that prayer the right indicator to open the doors of the Heavenly storehouse.

Where all the blessing is in the hands of God to pour into your house, and you must pray unto God. "Seek yea first the kingdom of God, and his righteousness all these things shall be added unto you" (KJV). God able to do anything we ask in his name in prayer, and prayer a powerful weapon against the enemy. I am glad it is the love of Jesus that cares for us, and God will allow us to fall down on our knees to pray unto the Father. Prayer can change things that look like it is impossible to do in a person life.

God can do all things far above than our minds, and eyes can even imaging. Example, "A certain man was there which had an infirmity thirty and eight years" (KJV). The situation looked impossible to man, and it is just right for God to handle. "Jesus saith unto the him, raise, take up thy bed, and walk" (KJV). God had turned the whole situation around in the man life and because he had faith in the Lord.

There have been times in my life feeling down, upset, and I will always turn to God in prayer for peace there is power in prayer. I learned to give thanks in all things that I go through in life. It is imperative for us to be thankful in all things, and always looking unto the Lord. The storm can't win, God has your destiny in his hands.

A dedicated pray life with God will keep you build up, and help you to go through the tribulations that may come your way. It is essential to seek God every day, and never stop praying. When you don't have a prayer life, you get weak along the way. The benefit of praying is to keep you in fellowship with God, faith, and motivation to stand. Prayer is your safety net to help keep you lifted above the storms that lie ahead without warning. It is imperative not to give up nor give in along the way, and just keep pressing your way through the storm. The storm can't win, God has your destiny in your hands.

It is imperative for you to pray before starting your day in the morning, and at night before retiring to bed. Prayer is a powerful tool to help you start a happy day, and a peaceful night before going to sleep to communicate with God in his present. When I pray it will allow me to feel the peace of God, and to listen to his voice. I learned that prayer would build a wall up against the enemy, and stop his plans.

The enemy has tried many times to make me think there is no hope and peace in my life. The power of prayer will change things, and God hands will defeat the enemy. The eye of the storm will try to gain force, and the situation may look a little dim. The omnipotent hands of God able to stop the turmoil in your life, and just keep laying at the feet of Jesus protected you. I was thankful God right there to see me through the storm, and test. The power of God is greater than any mountain, and there is nothing that can penetrate his anointing.

There is nothing God can't do upon the earth to overpower his works and love for us. Power is a force of action, energy, electricity, movement, authority, and control of any element that is on the earth. It is imperative to understand that when the supreme the Almighty King steps on board everything is subject to bow to God's command.

I was in the midst the cloudy storm Jesus lifted me up, and delivered me from the rushing wind, lighting that causing my life to be almost shipwrecked. God had another plan for my life, and he made the storm back up and behaved for his Glory. God had allowed the turmoil to cease, and not rip me apart but to take me into my destiny. "There is power in the name of Jesus" (KJV). God's sovereignty rests and ruled upon the earth. I had to pray and ask God for strength to endure the things try to hold me down in the storm. The storm can't win, God has your destiny in his hands.

I kept on praying, and God releases his power to help me go through the hardship and struggle that seems to be intolerable. There were sometimes in my life it looks to be in a blink, and nothing was going right. There was nothing else left for me but to call on God in the time of my trouble.

Sometimes the enemy will try to blow things up in your mind bigger than it appeared. The trick of the enemy is trying to distract you and get you discourage while going through in the storm.

You had your mind made up, and there was a way out the situation, and you did not know the day or hour God was going to step in to deliver you. Every moment, you had cried out looking for a breakthrough to come your way. I heard so much about the power of God, and how the Lord will saturate your heart, mind, and your Spirit. The enemy will try to sit back, and laugh throwing a stone. You may have asked yourself a question. Where is God?

I just believed that God would stretch forth his anointed hands to lift you above the head of your enemy. God is sitting, watching the plans of the enemy, and the Almighty King will dismantle the devil's weapons every time. The power of God in the midst the storm to bring peace, and to defeat the enemy. "No weapon that is formed against thee shall prosper; and every tongue that shall raise against thee in judgement thou shall condemn" (KJV).

The power of God's hand in the midst the storm to unlock the enemy to drop his weapon. The victory is now yours, and God will make the enemy leave you alone in the name of Jesus. God, said the battle won, and I had seen the power that lays the Lord's hands. There is no other greater than the Almighty King of King. The storm can't win, God has your destiny in your hands.

God was there all the time

You may have experienced a time in your life it seemed like everyone has walked away, and turned their back on you. In the darkest hour in the storm. Jesus is in the midst all the valley, despair, frustration, all the ups, and downs in life the world try to swing at you. There were times, I felt like could not trace God, and the Lord was there all the time just like a footstep in the sand. "Be strong and of good courage, fear not, nor be afraid of them: for the Lord thy God, it is that doth go with thee; he will not fail thee, nor forsake thee" (KJV).

There were times in my life things was rough, and it was hard trying to be strong in the storm. I had to look back over my life, and think things over the good always out weight the bad times. The roads may have seemed long, and just a glimpse no way out of the valley, and God reached way down to bring me out of the storm. The storm can't win, God has your destiny in his hands.

In the middle of my night, light is always shining through my window, and the darkest will disappear. God is always on the throne, and watching to make sure the storm leaves us alone, and the Lord's hands will defeat the enemy. "Be still and know that I am God" (KJV). There were times when the enemy tries to make you think no one care, and you are by yourself. The enemy will like to play a game of deception with the mind and try to bring depression, fear in your life.

You have to keep pressing forth and do not look back in the past in life. "I will lift mine eyes unto the hills, from whence cometh my help" (KJV). I will look to heaven, and believe my God is in control of my life. There is nothing every too hard for God to handle on the earth, and it is imperative to give all your cares unto the Lord.

PART- THREE

Placing your feet on a solid rock

walking on the earth every day is a joy and look around to see the beautiful creation God's hands had prepared for us. While on the journey you will always experience some issues no matter where the destination maybe sometimes in life. I have experienced some of the highways in life, and it was not always the right way to travel. Even the expedition is sometimes not confrontable, and it can be hard to go back to starting point. Sometimes life has a way of making you almost lose your balance sometimes, and fall.

It is hard sometime to get back up again, and you might face the same situation. "He brought be up out of a horrible pit, out of the miry clay, and set my feet upon a rock" (KJV). There different things in life causing you to almost stumble, and lose your grip while walking along to your destination. The storm can't win, God has your destiny in his hands.

God will reach way down and pick you up, and the Lord will lift your head above all the enemies that tried to block your path. I am so thankful God had looked beyond our faults, and see the needs in your life. Jesus is the rock that bigger, and taller any human that walks on the earth today. There are all different sides, and shapes of the nature rocks on the earth that can never match up to God.

The rock that I stand on is not like sink and sand smooth to slide in the direction which may cause you to fall, and get hurt. That rock is Jesus that allows us to be still through the storm that may try to take you out, and God will not let you fall on the ground. What rock will you lean on today? We will stand on that solid rock which is Jesus, and there nobody greater. God is the rock I now stand on today. The storm can't win, God has your destiny in his hands.

Jesus is a sure foundation, and when nothing else will seem to work out God is your solid rock. There have been times in my life I heard friends say girl I got you, and don't worry. They, are not always dependable when a tough time arrives in your life. The Master we serve is awesome filled with the authority lead us through the highest valley. Jesus is a rock that spreads wider than any ocean or mountains, and he can conquer any storm in our life. The storm can't win, God has your destiny in his hands.

I have traveled on vacation up in the mountains several times in the summer. Example, I saw a sign that says beware of falling rocks. The enemy will try to throw rocks at you, and make you fall. "When the enemy come in like a flood, the spirit of the Lord shall lift up a standard against him" (KJV). There is power in the name of Jesus, and does not matter the time it is Jesus on the way to rescue you. God has declared victory over the enemy on your behalf in the midst the battle. The storm can't win, God has your destiny in his hands.

You can never go around a big mountain of problems, and it is too huge for you to fix. God is the answer to any stumbling block moving it out of your way. God will allow us to stand on the word of Jesus Christ. It is imperative for us to move out of the way, and let Lord work. When the voice of God speaks everyone will obey the command, and vow.

There were times; I could see the enemy trying to set up traps in the storm and try to stop me from reaching my destiny. Every time the enemy thought he had you pinned in the count of three, and in the cave, there was no light to see your way through the valley. "For in the time of trouble he shall hide me in his pavilion: in the secret place of his tabernacle: shall he hide; he shall set me upon a rock" (KJV). Jesus is a sure foundation for you, and nothing can take you out of the Lord's hands.

I will always feel safe being in the arms of God, and nothing can harm me. It is essential to continue to stand on that solid rock, and you covered in the blood of Jesus. There is peace, and joy standing in faith while going through your daily life journey.

The rock, you can stand on can never be deceived, hurt, abused, trapped over in the mud, and pushed aside. The Lord will wipe every tear drop away from you, and give a new insight to find your destiny. Jesus is your rock, and he can move every road block that tries to hinder you from getting to your breakthrough. God did not allow the storms in our life to break us. The storm it is used as a vehicle to make you for that divine purpose God appointed.

Trying to stay on your journey

The journey on the right path will sometimes get challenging along the way. The enemy will always try to stop you from getting on the right road in life. Sometimes the enemy will compel you to make a detour, and go another way. "Thy word is a lamp unto my feet, and a light unto my path" (KJV). God is a bright light that always shines in our life, and will never dim no matter what kind of circumstances that lays ahead. You may have experienced yourself in a trouble situation, and you felt there was no way out. Sometimes, living your life on the edge, and trying to do things your way almost hitting the bottom. It was difficult trying to see, and it is complicated to see with no light.

God is awesome, loving in all his ways to wrap his arms around you while yet standing in the storm. It is like standing there in the crowded room with no light on to see around you. You will sometimes get confused trying to find the right door that leads you to your destiny. You will feel like you trapped behind the door. The storm can't win, God has your destiny in his hands.

Have you ever been inside of a place, and you did not feel comfortable? I have experienced not feeling relaxed in this quiet location, and it was strange emotions. I thought it was fun laughing with others, and did not feel shame. In the storm, there was no peace surrounding me, and I felt out of place.

When you have tried everything in our heart, and mind to fit in with the crowd, and it would not work. Example, I took a close look around, and it seemed like everything is ok in the room. Every moment was another deception from the enemy trying to keep stopping us from excelling. It is not the will of God for us to continue going back to the same place and there some doors meant to be close never open again. The enemy will try to keep pulling you in another direction.

The nature side of us can see a real light, and another part vision the darkness. Our hearts, sometimes tested and you can feel the pull in the heart., and there is no peace. It is a little complicated to shift your life into another lane, and head the right way. We will always need someone to steer us in the right direction. Sometimes our life can seem like a crossroad wondering which intersection road to take A, B C, or D. Traveling on this highway every individual will need to slow down up ahead and proceed with caution to stop make the right decision.

Sometimes you are trying to open the right door, and it is hard to tell the night from day. You may feel like a roller coaster, and it will keep you spinning in circles. It is imperative to proceed with cautions before moving forward, and not bumping into someone else in front of you.

You may still find yourself in the dark, and you need to make the decision before crossing the intersection for your life. Life is about making the precise preferences, and being happy. It is imperative to make correct choice, and doing the proper thing to get out of the rough places. Sometimes life may be filled with confusion, pain, shame, doubt, and disappoint you have to be determined to keep pressing your way, and never giving up find the right door. When you, can open the door, the sunshine will peek through the silver lining in your life.

Is this the right place?

One day, I was traveling, God spoke to me, and said you need to get on the correct path, and you need to follow me Jesus spoke, "I am the way the truth and the life" (KJV).

God was letting me know you are going in the wrong direction and turn from your ways.

God said, I am the road that you are looking for, and tried finding the answers you been searching for years. The other roads have been broad crowded along the way my daughter and no peace lays head on those highways. It is essential not to continue trying to do things your way. "For my thoughts are not your thoughts, neither are your ways" (KJV). Sometimes our thoughts are not right, and it is imperative we should always follow God.

It is essential for us to learn more about Jesus, and desiring to find peace the midst of everything we are going through in life. When we are trying to transition to another level in life, and it is not always that easy to do. "For we wrestle not against flesh, and blood. but against principalities, against powers, and against rulers of darkest of the world, against spiritual wickedness in high places" (KVJ).

There are times you want to get on the right road, and it feels like something is always trying to hold you back in your life. I did not know at that time there was warfare going on in my mind, flesh, and the spirit. God had his hands on me even in my early stages in life. "Before I formed you in the womb I knew you; before you were born I set you apart; I appointed you as a prophet to the nation" (KJV). We are already chosen even in our mother womb to follow and to do the well the Lord. Your life was already written out in the Master's plan to do the will of God. The enemy will constantly try to weigh you down, and block your destiny. The flesh has a desire to do things the right way, and please God at all time.

The enemy will not want you to tap into the anointing power of God, and live a sin free life. I knew "in my heart" there was something that kept trying to hold me cavity in my body, and soul. It is imperative to keep your mind focus on God and to find peace in the storm. The storm can't win, God has your destiny in your hands.

Sometimes you are laying there tossing, and turning all night trying to make the right decision along the way. You are at the point things seem a little difficult to handle in life. There was some people pretended they loved you, and yet betrayed themselves with jealous, scarf, and anger. It is imperative for you to hold on, and don't give up along the way. The storm can't win, God has your destiny in your hands.

Life may seem like a revolving door keep going around in a circle. You must remember look up no matter what the problem may be in life. "I will lift my eyes unto the hills whence cometh my help" (KJV). You must keep crying out to God, and believing that God will make away even when it does not look like there any hope.

It is imperative to keep praying get on the right road and live a different lifestyle and environment. You can feel when something is missing in your life, and you feel the loneliness yet still searching for something to fill that empty space. You have a desire to climb to the top, and you are still at the bottom level of the floor.

You have been on the bottom too long and ready to go up to another level to experience a greater flow in God. You have cried all the tears on your pillow at night, the pain, and you desire the heartache to vanish away from your life. God said, "I am the way the truth and the light" (KJV). I ask myself a question where is that road? God is letting us know he is the way, and come on follow the King of King on the right path. I heard a beautiful voice whispering in my ears come follow me. The storm can't win, God has your destiny in his hands.

Example, it is like a mother trying to show her child how to walk, and the baby keeps falling every time they attempt to make another step and again back on the floor. You may

fall get back up again like a baby walked for the first time.

There is a light shining closer to your feet, and the storm

rage you are wondering where is the path. Jesus is that

bright light waiting to shine around us when it seemed

everything else dim, lonely, and confusing in the world.

It is imperative to find the right light to shine in your life,

and not getting overwhelm with the other things trying to

distract you from the outside interruption. It is essential to

stand in that light, and never go back to the worlds

darkness. The brightness that appears in Jesus is so

beautiful, and it will sparkle forever in your life.

The storm will try to hold you down, and keep you under

the radar. There is nothing too hard that God can't solve in

your life. Every time, you were trying to get on the right

road there something always tries to block you. The

greatest light is Jesus that forever shine in your life, and

keep your life at peace. The light of God is brighter than

the stars, and it will never need a recharged or replaced by the hands of man. There are different types of lights in the world, example a spot light, fog light, flood light, porch light, bright light, pole light, and night light.

The nature lights can't outshine the light of Jesus, and it is everlasting that shines all over the world. We need the light of God to shine in our life during a difficult time and trying to make the right decision. When you receive Jesus in your life, and you had some struggle trying to get to the promising path filled with love and happiness. We must continue to get closer to God, and rejoicing in the name of Jesus for a new life.

I kept calling on the name of Jesus

It was imperative for us to find Jesus, and to desire peace in the midst the storm There is hope in God, and it is essential to call on Jesus, and everything will be alright just don't give up in the middle of the battle. It is important to have a relationship with God, and learning to communicate. Every time you feel lonely, depressed, and not sure if your directions you headed in the right place call on God. The storm can't win, God has your destiny in his hands.

The enemy always tried to block, and stop your progress most of the time. There were times the towel almost failed out of my hands, and nearly give up at the last minute. I heard a still small voice speak to me in wee hours of the night. "Call unto me, and I will answer thee, and shew thee great mighty things which thou knowest not" (KJV). The voice of God spoke to so clear in my bedroom that night, and I was happy to hear from the Lord. There was some situation that almost had me bound to my seat., and I did not understand how to handle the situation. I had to keep calling on the name of Jesus no matter how long it took to get my answer. There was a place in God I needed to reach my destiny, and learn the ways of God to seek his face get on the right path. Sometimes, we may feel like God had forgotten all about us, and you were left ship wreck with no hope. The storm can't win, God has your destiny in his hands.

God promised he would never fail you, and it is imperative just to keep calling on the name of Jesus. "Trust in the Lord with all your heart and lean not to your own understanding" (KJV). God wants us to depend on him in the time of your situations, and in the midst, everything you are experiencing just keep pushing to the finish line. The storm can't win, God has your destiny on his hands.

The enemy will try to make you believe it was a waste of keep calling on God. When you start seeking the face of God, and you will feel a shifting in the atmosphere the calmness will take place in your present. God is so awesome in his work, and never too late. It is to imperative keep calling on the name of Jesus every day.

When I call on the name of Jesus, something always happened in my life so awesome. Jesus name is the sweetie's name I know on the face of the earth. There are many names; we could call using our phone example, job, school, and the church. There is no other title that out weights the name of Jesus. Some days there may be things going on in your life, and you need someone to talk about your situation. You look around there is no one you can trust, and give an answer to your problem.

God will put you in place by yourself, and talk to him about your situation that you are facing in life. God will sit down beside you on your front porch or anywhere. You may just look around everything is quiet, and you did not know where to start with your words talking to God. The tears are flowing down your cheeks waiting on the Lord to move for you. We find ourselves asking God where is my friend when I need to talk them in my weakest hour? God spoke "Let not your heart be troubled: ye believe in God, believe also in me" (KJV). My mind had begun to feel at ease for a moment just hearing God speaking to me. God already told us not to get depressed about things going on around you, and just believe in him because the storm will pass over in your life

Sometimes it looks like things are about to fall apart at the seam, and Jesus will step in just in time. God said, "For in the time of trouble he shall hide me in his pavilion: in the secret place of his tabernacle shall he hide me: he shall sat me upon a rock" (KJV). It is imperative for us to understand the word of the Lord, and take God at his word.

My heart was filled with great joy, and it is the love I felt from God gentle arms embracing me at the time of distress. There is power in the name of Jesus, and just calling, believing everything is going to work out in your favor. Sometimes we can hear those spoken words, and still waiting for things to manifest itself in our life. The enemy will try to make you put your guards down, and put doubt in your heart. "Now faith is the substance of things hoped for the evidence of things not seen" (KJV). You must believe that God hear your prayer.

It is a blessing to call on God, and he will answer you when calling on the name of Jesus. Yes, it is awesome calling on Jesus, and he is never too busy, and you don't have to wait a few minutes or call back later. God is not like a man, and forget to answer you back, and you will not be on hold.

The direct call to Jesus is never a busy signal, and the connection is always easy to access to the line. It is imperative to stay connected to God and live a stress-free life. I found a friend in my sweet, and loving Savior that died on the cross for us. It is essential to plug into that main line, and never get cut off calling on Jesus name. The name of Jesus is just like a whisper sweet dreams, and the middle of the night while laying your head on a soft pillow.

I can feel a breath of fresh air in my room, and Jesus said the storm is defeated. I know just calling on that name Jesus is like a sweet-smelling fragrance in the atmosphere. The move of God in my present was a marvelous experience, and allowing Jesus to do some great things in your life. The storm can't win, God has destiny in his hands.

It is imperative for us to see God's Glory in the midst of our situations, and there is nothing too hard, nor unshakable for the Lord to do. God said, "He shall call upon me, and I will answer him: I will be with him in trouble; I will deliver him, and honor him" (KJV). God has told us many times to call on him, and it does not matter the day or night. It is an honor, and it is a privilege Jesus allows us to call him anytime with no charge.

There are different types of calls in the world to today example a call to duty, serve, honor, unity, and a call to peace. The appeal of Jesus is the best call to make in the situation in our life. It does not matter the part of the country you live God will be there for you. God is all loving and understands through every walk of life. There is no failure in God, and the connection is so powerful we can never get disconnected when calling Jesus name.

We have the permission from God to call anytime, and I will never get exhausted calling on Jesus name. The name Jesus alone has the connecting power turned on generate loved, peace, joy, hope. God will deliver your heart from pain, disappointment, and a lonely life. Jesus said the storm couldn't win, and you shall walk in your destiny there is nothing else to say, but Lord thank you.

God able to help you get on the right track, and do not look back to the past. God hands, is mightier than anyone in this world, and no other hand can overpower nor rule. It does not matter if the highway you are traveling, and it has three or four curves God can straighten it all out for your good. It is a blessing to see the hands of God that turn our path in the right direction and allow us to follow the correct journey to your destination.

We will continue to trust God even when things do not look so good in your direction. "In all thy ways acknowledge him, and he shall direct thy paths" (KJV). We sometimes will head in the wrong direction and had to thank Gods for the correct path to follow.

Sometimes a nature road is similar the real road that you had traveled on one time before in your life. It is imperative to understand there is something always a little different about every road you travel on. We may have traveled down some roads with high bumps, and pot holes in it along the way knowing God is on your side.

The hands of God had made another turn that causes us walk into the right path in the name of Jesus. "Trust in the Lord with all thine heart; and lean not unto thou own understanding" (KJV). The directions from God is always right information, and believing God said the storm couldn't win. It does not even matter how broad that path may seem, and God will always point you in the right direction.

The wisdom of God is so far above all the measure that anyone can ever image, and more the eyes can behold. Your visibility must remain clear every time to see the step God want to continue to lead you. It is essential to understand not letting go of God's hand like a parent want release their child's hand, and they wonder off in another direction. When God has a plan, and a purpose for your life it is imperative to follow the Master's instructions. It is essential to wait for God time frame, and walk there in the path of his righteousness for his name is the King of all the nations.

PART- FOUR

The King of Glory is here for you

The Lord is my rock the time of the storm, and I need a shelter to protect me. "Lift up your heads oh yea gate; and be yea lifted up, ye everlasting doors; and the King of glory shall come in" (KJV). The spirit of the Lord spoke to me in night hour while going through a great deal struggles, and God was talking to me and said I am here for you. The Lord has your hand don't look at the storm stay focus on God promises for you God had spoken to me again the King of Glory right here by your side to help you through every storm.

The tears were running down my face, and I looked towards heaven to say Lord thank you. I was so happy Jesus got my attention that night, and he came to see about me. God steps are never too short in the midnight hour and promised me to be right there in the midst my tears, pain, and heartaches. The storm can't win, God has your destiny in his hands.

I had begun to feel the hand of God wiping the tears from my eyes. I had felt the love, and the confront of Jesus with his arms wide open to hold me letting know he got me. King means that Jesus has the preeminence over all things that is on the earth. The hands of God had wiped away every pain, and scare in my life.

The hands of God will smooth all your heart, and calm all the doubt in your life. Your life had been shaken upside down, and you felt there was no hope. The King of Glory touched my hands and said come on let me guide you, and confront you. The King Glory is the great powerful one in all the earth and a loving creator. The man with nail scarred hands brought me out of my darkness into the marvelous light filled with joy.

I had never felt so loved before Jesus came into my life, and told me "take my yoke upon you, and learn of me; for I am meek and lowly at heart: and ye shall find rest unto your souls" (KJV). God wanted to teach us his way is the right direction for our life, and no other path. "For my yoke is easy, and my burdens are light" (KJV). The voice of God was made so clear to my ears that summer night. God had helped me find peace and love through his divine connection.

Taking your hands out of the situation

Sometimes in life, we have the intention of trying to help God out and move the situation to another level. What God had to let us know to move, and take your hands out of the issues. It seemed like your life was heading downstream in a dangerous place with no life guard to keep you from drowning in the storm. We as Christians want to process the speed up in our lives, and God is trying to get our attention to let it go. I had found myself questioning God about certain things going on in my life.

The question is sometimes we ask God why? God has a reason for everything that goes on in our life, and it is already predestinated. "And we know that all things work together for good to them that love God, and to them who are called according to his purpose" (KJV). God has a purpose and a plan to allow things happened in our life. There are times we do not understand the plan of God for our life. I had to learn for myself by trying to put my hands in the equation is not going make God go any faster.

It is important not to interrupt the move of God's hand, and wait let the Lord fix your situation. The reason why is not to slow the procedures down and submit the problem over in the Lord's hand. The Lord had spoken take your hands off the matter and leave it alone. It is imperative to understand God's orders to stop and move back it is essential to listen. Sometimes in life, the situations may get a little hard to bare, and you almost give up. The enemy will sometimes stick up his head trying to make you give up. "When the enemy comes in like a flood, the spirit of the Lord shall lift up a standard against him" (KJV).

The hands of God will fight your battle for you. God is giving you some instructions to follow take your hands off the problem, and let the Lord fight for you. I have learned in this walk with God that it is imperative to stand back and let God handle the situation. I have tried in the past try to stick my hands and help God out with my problem. God do not need any help with anything that is going in our life, and there is nothing too hard for God to fix for us. Your mind will make you think God is moving too slow, and the nature side of us want it done right that second. We must listen and be patient you can't hurry God.

"Ye shall not need to fight in this battle: set yourself stand ye still, and see the salvation of the Lord with you, O Judah and Jerusalem: fear nor be dismayed; tomorrow to go out against them: for the Lord will be with you" (K J V). It

essential to listen to God speak, and there is always a

reason for every decision made in the Master's plan.

Listening is an important skill to communication, and

follow the direction. It is God that wants us to rest, and rule

over our life with all power and Glory on the earth.

"And Jehoshaphat bowed his head with his face to the

ground: and all Judah and the inhabitants of Jerusalem fell

before the Lord and worshipping the Lord" (K J V). God

want all the praises and the Glory in the earth. The power

of God will move any mountain or stubbing block out of

the way in Jesus name.

God had warned us to move out of the line of the battle

and put the situation in the Lord hand. It is imperative to

understand God when the word spoken move out of the

way and it is already declared the storm you can't win, God

has your destiny in his hands. There are some situations in

your life only God can handle, and it is out of our control, and our hands not quick enough to outbox God.

The unlimited power of God's hands able to knock the enemy out with one punch. It will not matter how upset we get the issue is still the same, and you can't overturn it yourself. God is King of King, and the Lord of Lord over the entire universe ruler of everything. I had to take my hands out of all my problems and gave it to God let him fight for me.

Every day with Jesus is sweeter than the day before, and allowing God to handle the problems makes life a lot easier to live. It is imperative to understand that we can't change any situation in our own. God will change things, and you have to keep the faith never let go of the Lord hands. "For we wrestle not against flesh, and blood, but against principalities, against powers, against the rulers of darkness of this world, against spiritual wickedness in high places"

(K J V). The storm can't win, God has your destiny in his hands.

There are sometimes opposing moments that the enemy may use someone, and they will try to fight against you. You have to hold your peace and let the Lord fight the battle. It is imperative not to put yourself in the middle situation, and mess things up. You put your hands in the circumstance it will block God from taking care of the problems.

God is an all seeing, and knowing God that can shift every storm in another direction. Ask yourself a question can God turn that storm into another path? The answer is yes, and the situation will cease when Jesus step on board and take full control. God has the power to do anything in his will to cause a storm to stop.

The enemy will try to come, and try to make the picture look bigger than what it appears. The devil will come, and try to make you forget about trusting God with your situation. It is essential not to get depressed over your problem, and trust the Lord with all your heart.

It is imperative to make the right choice let God be in control, it is the best solution for you. Life is sometimes filled with so many ups, and down we never know what tomorrow may bring in your path. "Nay, we are more conquerors through him that loved us" (KJV). The storm will seem a little heavy sometimes just lift your head up God got you in the palm of his hands. The problem appears to keep slipping another direction, and you are holding on through all turmoil. The storm can't win, God has your destiny in his hands.

I refuse to give up, and no need for a pity party in the battle. There is no reason for anyone to allows frustration, stress to invade your space. It is essential to totally surrender everything unto God because he is the only way out of your situation. Sometimes your life felt like it was

spending out of control, and you had to let go and let God
handle that big task. It is imperative to understand while
totally surrender until God allows you to live more peaceful
in the will of God. Remember it is important to take your
hands outs of the situation and let God do it. The storm
can't win, God has your destiny in your hands.

Keeping your praise through the storm

There is rough moment sometimes in our life, and
keeping a praise in the storm can be a challenge. It is
imperative to keep your praise during the darkest hour of
the night, and holding on to God's hands. God is right there
with us, and man or woman will not be close by your side
like Jesus.   There is nature storm we may need an umbrella
to try stop from getting wet and before coming inside the
house.

You will face challenges in your life and it is imperative
to hold on to God. Once you have reached to the top of the

mountain and you have overcome the storm in your life. "My lips will shout for joy when I sing praises to you; my soul also which you have redeemed" (K J V). The storm can't win, God has your destiny in his hands.

My soul will continue to rejoice in the Lord even in the midst the trails, and I will still praise his holy name. "When you pass through the waters, I will be with you; and through the rivers it shall not overwhelm you; when you walk through the fire you shall not be burned, and the flame shall not consume you" (K J V). It does not matter how sever that storm seems to try a shake, rock, and roll you God has the storm under control in your life. The storm can't win, God has destiny in his hands.

I will always praise God with my lips and offer a sacrifice praise unto the Lord. Sometimes a nature storm like a tornado, hurricane, flooding, earthquake, and it will cause some individuals to lose power, homes, cars, and sometimes lives. The enemy will try to come and rob your joy, peace, anointed power through our praising God. "The joy of the Lord is my strength" (K J V). It is imperative not to lose sight in praising God during your storms that may rage.

There is no need of complaining about the situation, and it is imperative to allow God in the control room. God can stop the storm in your life and the peace to appear rest upon you. Why do we find ourselves sometimes complain about things, and it is out of out of your control? Why we try to change circumstances that are way above our head? It is essential to stop complaining and trust God with every battle that sent out by the enemy. God has the power to do anything and never fail.

It is imperative to understand a spiritual walk means to be filled with the Holy Spirit and it is the right passageway with God. You have to trust God, and believing he will take you through the storm with the victory. One day I was sitting down on my bed and thought about some things and began to realizing the best way to overcome a troublesome storm is to praise your way out. "Praise the Lord with harp: sing unto him with psaltery and instrument of ten strings" (K J V). The praises of God will allow you to get a break through from the storm, and the blessing of the Lord will come down.

I will never forget a time in my life, and I didn't have good transportation, and money to purchase another car. I woke up that morning, and God gave me a word and said I will bless you with new transportation. I began to praise God and trusted the word that the Lord release to me in the spirit that Wednesday morning.

I was continually praising God for my blessing, and believe with all my heart. I had fallen on my knees and asked God to shows me where to get my car. I had finished praying and got up off my knees God reveals where to go to get my car. I looked up toward heaven and said where is the money to purchase. God had spoken to me the favor already granted for you just go and purchase your car. I had

driven up to the right location just like God told me. I had

faith in my heart, and the favor already spoke over me. I

believe my blessing was waiting for me on that lot.

The owner of the car looked at me and said lady here is

the keys to the car, and go ahead drive it home. God had

given me the favor just like he told me in my prayer room.

I had faith in God, and praises on my lips uplifting the

name of Jesus. My old car had a lot problem and needed

another car. The storm that appeared many years ago

couldn't win, and God has your destiny in his hands.

God will bring you out without a shadow of a doubt. We

have to praise God for every situation in our life and does

not matter how long you been in the storm. The

compliment and the faith in our heart will go way above the

circumstances in your life. We must praise God no matter

how impossible the situation may seem to appear before

you.

The enemy will try to draw a big picture, and try to make us doubt God in the midst the storm. We have to praise God for all of his faithfulness, and keeping his promise. God will take care of you in your storm, and just give him the praise. The praise on your lips is stronger than the storm before my eye, and the Glory of God defeat all the turmoil. The storm can't win, God has your destiny in his hands.

We have to give God the highest praise Hallelujah, singing and shouting the victory to the all Mighty King. It is essential to understand when the worship offered up to the Lord healing, deliverance, miracle, signs, and wonders will take place. Praising God is an important weapon through prayer to fight the enemy, and decree the victory. It is imperative to praise the Lord before your breakthrough introduce in your life. The storm can't win, God has your destiny in his hands.

The power of God's praises is the right tool to use through a big or small storm. Example, riding along in your car a bad rain storm had come up, and you will need to turn on your windshield wiper to see how to drive. Sometimes in the in the middle of a good storm the rain will come down hard or slow, and sometimes the rain will appear to be slated coming down.

It does not matter how hard the storm is moving in your life. The important thing is to stay focus, and do not lose hope in the battle, and trust God. There are other storms that my try to overpower you. You must reach back to pull up a praise to help see yourself clearly out of the turmoil.

There is victory in the praise, and it will renew your strength. The enemy is afraid of the name of Jesus, and the praises from your lips. God is so awesome, and the Lord allows trails to take place to help expand our faith level in the Lord.

When we praise God, it changes the storm to another direction in your life. "And being fully persuaded that, what he has promised, he was able also to perform" (K J V). I had been truly convinced in my heart God can deliver you out of the storm. The storm can't win God has your destiny in his hands.

Praising God is a effective weapon to fight the enemy while going through the storm, and it will help bring forth deliverances. It is imperative to praise God before a storm even occur in your life, and when a disaster trying to take place on your grounds. It is imperative to praise God no matter what situation look like in your life continue to give him all the Glory.

Your praying, and faith trusting God will bring you out every time. There is nothing too hard for our God to handle, and the praises will out weight the storm. Praises is what I do, and it will stir up your faith, and strength to bring forth your deliverances. God able to allow the dark clouds to disappear, and bring a brighter sun light in your life through praises.

The storm we are facing in life could not come not unless God allowed us to go through that test for a purpose. The situation God placed before us is working something out for our good, and it is essential to go through the process. Yes, the storms did come in your life and still survived through it all.

There were times you may felt like given up but God that lived on the inside of us held on to the Master's hands. We may have to lay flat on the floor before God crying asking to please help us go through the turmoil. You feel the storm is blowing in the midnight night hour and the winds blowing stronger at the door, and thought you could not see your way in the storm. "I can do all these through Christ that strengthenth me" (K J V). The storm can't win God has your destiny in his hands. It is imperative to trust the King of King the Lord of Lord all power in his hands.

Broken in the storm

Sometimes storms will come to break down and shake up things into another position. The storm you had encountered in your life did not come to break us down altogether it began to process you in the right place God desire. A relationship you may have experienced a broken heart and it have cause a storm to appear in your life.

The turmoil has erupted into flame your heat with sorrow, anger, disappointment. God able to put your heart back together again through that storm, and it is imperative to give the problems over to the Lord. "Cast thy burden upon the Lord, and he shall sustain thee: he shall never suffer the righteous to be moved" (KJV). God wants us to give all of problems to him let the King of Glory handle your storm "He heals the health the broken in heart, and bindeth up their wounds" (KJV). The Lord able to put your broken hearts back on the wheel and make us over again for his glory. The storm can't win, God has your destiny in his hands. Have you ever asked God why? There so much confusing going on in your mind, and you were trying to erase the pain. The storm comes to make us and not to break us. The storm can't win, God has your destiny in his hands.

Every problem we face in life God will turn it into a stepping stone to process us, and God will get all the Glory. God wants us to keep the faith through our test, and to make us strong. God hands had turned the storm that tried to take you out, and could not see in the midst the turmoil in your life.

I have sat on your porch many of days crying, and wiping the tears from my eyes saying life not supposed to work like this Lord. We want to know from God where did I go wrong in my life? I found out that life does not always go the way we had planned it to go, and things happen for a reason.

The storm will come to try to break us all the way down to the ground and never get back up. There was broken relationship in the storm, and was trying to put it back on the right track. The devil meant some things for evil, and God will work out for our good. Sometimes a natural storm will taper off for a little while to relax in it, and enjoy the bright sunshine. The storm can't win, God has your destiny in his hands. I am glad that God is on our side, and the storm want break us it come to help make us stronger in the Lord.

There sometimes turmoil will pop ups uninvited issues in our life, and it may cause a lot of heartache pain, disappointment. The storm is a tool to help us to get to the right place with God. A nature storm can break down power lines, trees fall and cause a lot of serious problems, and clean up the mess made in the neighborhood. The pieces in our life seemed to scatter everywhere, and it is hard trying to find all the right pieces to put back together in our life.

When broken, and it is hard to find the pieces to put things back in the same matter. It is imperative to understand putting things back together won't be the same, and it is complicated to do. Relationships are sometimes hard to mend together because of the loss of love, and trust. God is love, and he first loved us first, die for our sins on the cross now that is the real compassion.

Our heart had been broken by someone that meant a lot, and share so many things together along the way. The person that was so close to your heart betrayed you and broke the seal of trust. Have you ever been betrayed by someone you loved? I believe a lot of us have been left in that storm and left us heartless.

It is not a good feeling someone you loved, and trust had turned their back on you in the middle of a storm. There may have been a time in your life someone said I got your

back, and you look around they no longer there as

promised. I have experience that storm in my life, and the

wind was blowing in your life. The storm can't win, God

has your destiny in his hands.

   The broken heart was a stepping stone to finding my

destiny and waiting in the Lord. "God will never leave you

nor forsake you" (K J V). The love of God is pure, and

never contaminated with other germs, and it is clean. God

is love, and the all mighty King gave us the right to the tree

of life filled with love, peace, happiness, and total healing

for our heart that was broken. "For so loved the world he

gave his only begotten son, that whosoever believe in him

shall not perish, but have everlasting life" (KJV). There is

no greater love than Jesus laid down his life us on the cross.

   Our heart was broken in the storm with rejection, denied,

repudiation, and we are never alone cause God always by

your side every step of the way. Relationships are just like building blocks it takes the time to build it up to trust, love, and communication. There will be questions in your mind can you ever pick up the pieces, and start over on another page with your life? The answer is yes, God able to erase every scare that enemy try to leave on your life. The storm can't win, God has your destiny in his hands. It is imperative to continue to try keeping yourself in the right perspective, and never give up.

Life has so much to offer you, and it is essential not to stay in the storm with your heart broken. Sometimes the heart is yearning trying to find the right direction to go in life. "Jesus answered, I am the way and the truth and the life" (KJV). The heart is beating and broken trying to find comfort to ease the brokenness from the relationship seem impossible to repair.

You have tried everything else, and nothing seem to alleviate the pain for just for a moment. "He healeth the broken in heart, and bindeth up their wounds" (KJV). God can fix the heart that broken in the storm.

I began to look at how a mirror can fall off the wall, and break in scattering into hundreds of pieces, and will never be able to put it back together again. We know there is no way a mirror scattered into that many pieces will never be fixed. Our everyday life has many daily activities, and it is imperative to stay healthy to complete our journey.

We know that our emotions come from the brain signals, and it tells the heart what to do. The heart is an important access to the body it's essential to stay healthy and live a stress- free life. It is imperative to be strong to do the extraordinary things every day, and not to be weighed down with stress. How do I get those broken pieces in my heart fixed?

"The Lord is nigh unto them that are of broken heart; and saveth such be of a contrite spirit" (KJV). God able to help us that brokenness, and free us from some painful issues that had us bound. God spoke and told me he able to fix that scattered heart that needed repair. We sometimes try everything to take away our hurt, and disappointment.

The heart is a tender spot inside of our body, and it is very easy too bruise and it must be handled with special care. "Take my yoke upon you, and learn of me; for I am meek and lowly in heart: and ye shall find rest unto your souls" (KJV). The word of God will bring life to your soul, and it is imperative to believe the Lord with our whole heart. It is essential to rest in God, and don't give up on your healing. The storm can't win, God has your destiny in his hands.

"Trust in the Lord with all your heart, and lean not to thine own understanding" (KJV). Somethings are not always the way it seemed to appear, and the enemy will try to deceive your heart. It is imperative to protect the heart from doubt, lies, bitterness, and confusing. The storm can't win, God has your destiny in his hands.

It is essential to keep your minds stayed on the Lord, and God will keep us content in our hearts, and minds. The devil will try to pretend this is the right relationship to walk into, and everything is going to be okay. The enemy will come in different ways to make you think that God sent this person, and it will sometimes cause our life to be tossed upside down.

It is imperative not just look at the person from the outward appearances, and we think they are the right one for us. The beginning of the relationship things seemed to flow along very well, and somewhere down the road, and we hit a bump. The enemy will try to use anything to destroy God's people in the storm.

Yes, the turmoil that came in our life was a light storm. The storm can't win, God has your destiny in his hands.

We sometime will ignore the alarm signal sent right to us, and decide to continue in the relationship. God has been showing us warning signs all along, and we ignored it every time there was flag held in front of our face. The relationship had begun to hit rock bottom, and we look for a quick way out, the situation. Sometimes the enemy will try to send different kinds of storms in our life example, job, home, relationships, business, and finances. The storm can't win, God has your destiny in his hands.

It is imperative too realized, God did not put you in that place. Sometimes we choose not to listen to warning signal from the beginning of the relationship. Sometimes we are in the world get involved in relationships for so many different reasons and not thinking things out before making the right decision in our life. Sometimes our hearts are feeling, and thinking on the wrong level at that time. God reached out his hands to me, and place me under his protection.

The first relationship we need to establish is with Jesus as our personal savior. The real foundation to be laid in our life should be God, and everything else will fall in line. The pain inside was like a deep wound and cuts down to the marrow of bones that kept bleeding for many years. My heart was sick, and it needed to be heal from the scars, cuts, even a bandage could not cover it all up. There were no medications, pain pills, sleeping pills, alcohol, and other things could take away the pain. A voice spoke, "Come unto me, all ye heavy laden, and I will give you rest" (KJV). God was speaking to my heart letting me know this load too heavy for you to carry, and give the problem to me. The storm can't win God has your destiny in his hands.

There may have been a time in your life, and you felt like can't take it. You said something got to change for me right now Lord. God knows when we are right at the end of our rope and couldn't handle no more pain. The heart is very sensitive, and God knows all about us, and the great creator that made every human on the earth. "Call unto me, and I

will answer thee, and shew thee great and mighty things

which thou knowest not" (KJV). We will sometimes cry

out unto God to help us through the storm, and show us the

right direction to take in life. The storm can't win, God has

your destiny in his hands.

I ask God to come into my life and fix my broken heart.

God let me know that very hour he was the way, and he

will deliver me from all my problems. My mind, and heart

was made up to try Jesus to help fix my broken heart in the

storm. God was already waiting with his arms wide open,

and give all my burden unto the Lord. Sometimes, we are

trying to figure things out ourselves and make a bigger

mess. I started giving my issues unto God's hands, and

immediately I had begun to see things working better for

me.

It is imperative to release all your problems unto God,

and let him do the fixing for you. I had to realize keeping

my hands in the situation cause God's hands to be blocked, and not able to give me an instant breakthrough. God able to do all things except but fail. God wanted me to get my hands out of the way, and Jesus did not need my help.

It was not clear to me from the beginning trying to fix things on my own was not working, and I was only making a bigger mess. There are some complicated issues can 't never be completed by man because it is above our control. Even in the nature eyes of man or woman, we can never know where each piece fit in every slot. Only God able to repair the broken heart, and put it all back together in fine tuning. God is a heart regulatory, and man can't go beyond the Lord's ability, strength and power. God is a healer and the powerful one that sat high on the throne. The storm can't win, God has your destiny in his hands.

Lord Give Me a New Heart

I had to bow down on my knees to ask God for a new heart, and take out this stone heart that scattered into thousands of pieces. It is impossible to see out of a mirror that broken into thousands of pieces. The solution to a broken mirror is to buy another one to see yourself in it and finish getting dress.

It is imperative to understand when our hearts are not correct it causes unpleasant words to come out of the mouth. The heart is not right it may cause angry, stress, bitterness, disagreement, confusing, and gossip. God able to take out the stony heart, and give us a new heart filled with love, peace, righteousness, and a desire to serve God.

The new heart will teach us how to love our enemy and our friends. God able to purify our heart, and make peace with all men and women. The new heart has the right beat to connect now, and allow God to open your eyes to a bright future. The old stony heart does not want you to have a good life and be free in Christ Jesus.

How can I get a new heart from God? There is a way in the nature realm man can transplant a new heart into a patient, and survive the procedure. The doctors will take out a weak heart because it may be filled with diseases faded, and replace it with a reverberated heart from a donor.

God said, "A new heart will I give you, and a new spirit will I put within you: and I will take away the stony heart out of your flesh, and I will give you a heart of flesh" (KJV). God able to take out that old heart that been batter in the storm. The King of Glory will come in our life. The storm can't win, and God has your destiny in his hands. God will give us a pure heart it is no longer dirty, and repented totally surrender to the Lord. We have a heart now that is full of love, and compassion for my brothers and sisters. The Lord can make you all over again, and free the broken heart filled with pain, and resentment. "And that ye put on the new man, which after God is created in righteousness, and true holiness" (KJV). The new heart God has given us the power to talk, walk, and live right in our new life. It is essential to let God have his way in your life and get free from all the doubt, fear, and negative responds you have encounter.

It is imperative today to allow God to give you a new heart, and it does not matter if you are rich, poor, nationality, social status, or ethnical background. It is essential to let God give you a new heart, and it will make a big difference in your life. The new love that God will place down inside cause you to love your enemy, and a greater desire to help people. The new heart God will allow you to speak victory. The storm can't win, God has your destiny in his hands.

The new heart will cause us to go into the church with a praise on our lips and worshipping God Holy name, and all the praises belong to King Jesus. The new heart is a powerful transformation that has taking place on the inside from the Master's hands. The heart filled with an inner peace, and you will never feel lonely, cold nor broken about the cares of the world. The heart was scattered in pieces, and now renewed by hands of the King of King. It is beyond any man thought how God turns a hard heart into love and cut out the old one with his powerful hands.

"God created man in his own image, in the image of God created he him; male and female created he them" (KJV). The human heart was supposed to be design like a mirror created after God's own heart. We are called to walk, and talk in the same manner to love God, and his people. It is essential to continue show our love before God, and the community, family, friends with all due respect. The heart is free to love once a transformation in us with a pure heart, and the right spirit.

A change in our hearts must come through God, and we can't do this ourselves deliverance from the yoke of bondage in our heart. We have a complete change in our heart it needs a transformation "And he came into all the country about Jordon, preaching the baptism of repentances for the remission of sin" (KJV). Jesus has come to make the crooked ways straight, and change to a new life. It is being born again washed in the blood of Jesus, and to receive a pure heart like God.

A spiritual healing will take place in our heart. God will present a surgery of his own to give us a new heart to love, and to give praise unto his name. The spirit of God will enter the hearts, and God will free us from sin to walk in the boldness of Jesus Christ with a new heart.

It is imperative to stay in the will of God, and love one another without jealousy, envious, disrespectful, hate and without resentment found among us. Our heart must be pure, and kind to helping people. There are some people without families, homeless, sick, poor, prison, hungry, and they are looking for someone to show love from a pure heart. It is imperative to keep our new heart in the right spirit with God and worship his holy name. The storm can't win, God has your destiny in his hands.

The God of our salvation has a kind heart unto all man, nature and we the people must do likewise. The heart is full of joy, and peace can help other that are going through a crisis. It is imperative the heart of woman or man is subject to the feelings other individuals in need. The storm can't win, God has your destiny.

The spirit of God will witness to the heart, and desire to help take care of God's people. God have people with real heart support others without any cost and only present their love. A person heart that filled with hate unthankful, impurity and skepticism of another people are not able to help individuals to reach their destiny.

"I will praise thee with up righteousness of heart, when I shall have learned thy righteous judgement" (KJV). My mind and heart now right with God to help others that are struggling along the way in life. The storm can't win, God has your destiny in his hands.

God has now made us disciples to help encourage the young, and the old trying show our love and peace in Jesus name. There are some people in the world today filled with hate, violence, troubled nation, and there are some people need love. There is no one in this world should be sad, and we should give a word of encouragement with a kind heart. There are some still in the storm that needs rescued and embraced with the love of Jesus. The storm can't win, God has your destiny on his hands.

It is imperative to always to make a person feel good about themselves and never look down on a man or woman less you support picking them up. It is essential to show a person you care by help lifting the load off their shoulder, and praying for them. The new heart God has given us to do things for individuals with a cheerful core and to be thankful and bless others. The heart filled with love is priceless, and can never measure beyond anything on the earth.

The best feeling in our heart helping someone else, and never look for anything in return. The new heart God place in us is supposed to give to love and look out for someone in need. The new heart will not turn their back on someone need a place to sleep or eat. The heart will say I love you let me a blessing to you. The storm can't win, God has your destiny in his hands

The Power of Praise Overturns the Storm

There are so many things we can give God praise for today, and worship his Holy name. Sometimes in life things will feel a little rough on the edges to cope with everyday living in society. A person life is filled with many responsibilities and trying to juggle life with all the ups and down it brings in the home.

It will feel like sometimes our backs are against the wall, and there no way out of the storm. The enemy will try to come and bring distractions, and try to cut off your praises and worship unto the Lord. We will sometimes even listen to gospel music to try to block the storm waving war in your head.

Sometimes you try to press through all the mess and offer up a sacrifice of praise unto God. The enemy will seek to put, fear, doubt, weary in your heart to waver you about trusting God with your situation. The spirit of wondering will try show up. Do God, love me enough to come, and see about me midst of the storm? Yes, God will come to our rescue any place and anytime.

The enemy will come to try put all kinds negative ideas in your heart, and mind. Sometimes we are pledge with wrong thoughts, and thinking that God does not love us enough to see about us in the time of trouble. The enemy will try to make you think God is too far away, and don't hear you call his name.

These are the trick, and snares of the enemy when you in the storm. You, sometimes will feel like it an uphill journey, and you took two steps backwards while losing some family, home, and the tears flowing on your pillow at night, tossing, turning in the storm. You must turn up your praise in the storm. The storm can't win, God has your destiny in his hands.

It is imperative to keep our minds on Jesus, and not to focus your eyes on the things around you. "But when he saw the wind boisterous, and he was afraid; and beginning to sink, he cried saying Lord save me" (KJV). Peter walked out in the water, and fear gripped his heart.

Peter took his mind off Jesus, and Peter was afraid of the things going on around him the wind blowing and the storm. Peter heart was filled with fear and almost drown in the storm. The enemy will try to do God's people the same way to lose focus. It is imperative to keep our eyes looking on Jesus and continue to give God all the Glory. We have to keep our hearts, minds before God, trusting, and praising his holy name. The storm can't win, God has your destiny in his hands.

There is power in the name of Jesus, and no other name can overrule in the earth. God wants our praises, worshiped in the present of his Glory to abide in our life every day. It is imperative to keep our eyes focus on Jesus every day to maintain our joy. "The joy of the Lord is our strength" (KJV). It does not matter what we are going through in life God will give us strength to go through it every step of the way. It is imperative to keep an intimate relationship with God and fulfill our joy. God wants our true worship, and praise from our lips to the all Mighty King with all his Glory.

Oh, when we praise God it will make the enemy push back all the corruption, and stop the assaults. The spoken falsifications against the people of God will stop in Jesus name. We are worshipping unto God, and the enemy must flee. The devil can't stand the praises, and it will cause the devil to shake at the name Jesus. God able to hold us up in the storm, and Jesus will fight our battles big or small it does not matter. Jehoshaphat was going through a battle, and God told him not to fight. The can't win, God has your destiny in his hands.

God stood up in the battle for Jehoshaphat and defeated the enemy because God commanded his people to praise his name. "And they began to sing and praise, the Lord set ambushments, against the children of Ammon, Moab, and Mount Seir, which were come against Judah; and they was smitten" (KJV). God has the power over the enemy, and the people of God gave praises they won the battle. The storm can't win, God has your destiny in his hands

It is essential to focus on God, and never keep looking at ourselves all the time continue praising the name of the Lord. The world that we live in sometimes will try to bring some distraction around us. We can't focus on the storm and it is imperative to stay grounded in the word of God. It is essential to understand the storm brought to you, and God able to bring you through it.

God wants our attention, and lift him up allow the Glory of the Lord to bless our lives. Sometimes the enemy will seek to bring confusion in your mind, and heart which will cause you to get out of the will of God. God is always worthy of all our praises, and bring forth the blessing of the Lord. "And my tongue shall speak of thy righteousness and of thy praise all the day long" (KJV). It is essential to give God praises from our lips and continue to lift his name up.

The Lord will bring us to a place, and with servility, and depend on Jesus to help us through the storm. We need to continue to give God the praises to the High King of the whole universe, and all the power lays in his hands. There is nothing too hard for God, and everything is subject to the name of Jesus.

"O come let us sing before the Lord: let us make a joyful noise to the rock of our salvation" (KJV). God is awesome in all his ways, and nothing can break down the arms of the Lord. I will continue to give all the praises, and the Glory of God shall rise above the head of the enemy. We are God's people don't continue grumbling, and refutation ways in our heart. Your praying is not in vain crying, and the contradiction about your problems. It is imperative to understand God eyes in every place searching the hearts, and minds of his people. God will see the storm before it gets near us and knows the strength, and the Lord will protect you.

God is about love, and always showing his powerful influences towards his people, and desiring the best for everyone. When we keep our minds on Jesus, it is easier to stay in focus, and praising God. The devil will always try to distraught your journey and will try to make you stop serving God. The storm can't win, God has your destiny in his hands.

Yes, we will go through storms in life, and the problem is not always big as it appears, and the enemy will seek to make you give up. God will give his people victory over every problem or struggle they may be facing in life.

The storm can't win God has your destiny in his hands God has done great things in our life, and it is imperative to continue to praise God Holy name. It is essential to understand God has already defeated the storm before we see it coming in our path. "Bless the Lord oh my soul, and forget not all his benefits, who forgives all your iniquity; who heals all your diseases, who redeems your life from the pit, who crowns you with steadfast love and mercy" (KJV). It is essential to understand that God is on our side, and he will fight our battles for us never turn away from God.

When we are praising God, it will open a stream of blessings to flow in our lives, the power of God rules over the earth. The power of God will bring about changes into your heart in the name of Jesus. It is essential to learn when the praises go up the blessing will come down.

The word of God tells us "And at midnight Paul and Silas prayed, and sang praises unto God: and the prisoners heard them" (KJV). The praises of God were sent up, and the deliverance came forth in the midst of their tribulation. "Suddenly there was a great earthquake, so that the foundations of the prison were shaken, and immediately all the doors were opened, and every one's bands were loosed" (KJV). God had a plan to release Paul and Silas through the

storm, and the devil could not stop the breakthrough. The
storm can't win, God has your destiny in his hands.

God had made a special house call on that night to do a
roll call for Paul and Silas deliverances. It is awesome
when the power of God shifts the storm in another
direction, and the room filled with peace everlasting joy.
The power of God is a strong tower, and what man may
think is impossible, and it is possible with God.

There is no question what God can do in our life today.
There is never anything too hard for God, and we must
have the faith to belief in Jesus name. We own all the
Praises to God with our whole heart, and our mind stayed
on Jesus. It is imperative to keep our spirit renew in the
presence of the Lord. We have to worship his holy name
together in the fullness of joy.

We are God's children choose by his Holy hands to
Praise and Worship his awesome name. "Create in me a

clean heart, O God and renew the right spirit within me"
(KJV). David was a man that loved the Lord, and enjoyed
praising his Holy name, and he wanted to make sure his
heart was right before God. It is essential to make sure our
heart is right before God, and in his present to always give
him the Glory. The praises from our lips will always invite
God in our Present with his Glory. "But O thy art holy, O
thou that inhabitest the praises of Israel" (KJV). We are
God's people, and he desire for us to give him all the Glory
bless it be the name of Lord.

The power of God will bring forth blessing to overflow
in your life today, and our hearts will be fill with Praises.
God is reminding us to watch him move in the midst of us
and bring forth awesome worship, and manifest in God's
his Glory upon the earth. We will sing praises with our lips,
and shout unto the Lord with a new song. "I will bless the
Lord at times his praises shall continually be in my mouth"
(KJV). It does matter how hard the storm is blowing in

your life. We shall always sing with a sweet melody from

our heart, and God will listen to all the sweet sounds

flowing in his ears when we give him the Praise.

There are times we must speak affirmative action in our

life and watch God will move for us. Sometimes in your

life there are different obstacles that try to stop your flow

with serving God to the fullness. You keep pushing your

way through the storm, and don't give up. The storm can't

win, God has your destiny in his hands.

God able to lift us up from the by worshipping his Holy

name with praises on our lips. The praises, and worship

will break every chain from sickness, financial struggles,

marriage, family, business, home, and jobs. It is imperative

to keep the sacrifice of praise in our heart, and magnify the

name of the Lord. God able to fight for his people, and just

show forth the praises of God. It essential to understand

God has already put his seal on it, and the victory won over the storm. The storm can't win God has your destiny in his hands.

It does not matter how the situation got started, and God able to defeat every storm in your life. When we are praising God, it releases strength to you to go own in life, and not to give up cause God able to bring you through your battle. Example, when we put our brakes on trying to drive the car it will not go forward cause the brakes are placed on to stop. When we take our foot off the brake it will release the car to go forth. The turmoil in your life just temporary give it to God, and watch God will move for you. The storm can't win, God has your destiny in his hands.

PART- FIVE

You are never a lone

Sometimes there is a situation we can't change, and it seems like you are all alone right by yourself. We are not alone because God is always in the midst us even while we are sleeping in the midnight hours. God has promised, he will be with us at all time, and when we feel like we can't trace his present in front of us God is still with you. It is imperative to understand God is always right there no matter what circumstances may pop up in your life. I have experienced some close calls in my life.

You are never alone even when your love ones not around you, God is still right there by your side. "There shall not any man be able to stand before thee all the days of thy life: as I was with Moses, so I will be with thee: I will not fail thee nor forsake you" (KJV). The storm may look a little dark sometimes in your life, but we are not alone God is with you through the battles.

The storm you may be facing can never predict how long it will last. God is your Meteorologist telling you the storm can't win, and God has your destiny. Sometimes our eyes can be spiritual impaired not being able to see or feel the supernatural move of God. God's arms never too short we can't feel his present all around in the midst you. God is always on time, and never late concerning the needs of his people. It is imperative to walk in the present of God, and we can see the hands of God move upon our life.

It is essential never to feel like God don't see or hear you. God already know our heart. Your heart will sometimes get a little weighted because of the cares of the world that trying to press you down. God will never abandon you in the midst your hardship, sickness, suffering, and pain in your time of trouble. We can never put a price on God's love that he gives to us every day, and we should always continue to praise the name of Lord forever.

It does not matter where it may appear too dark in the midst the situation in your life God will always guide you in the right direction. "Even there shall may hands lead me, and thy right hand hold me" (KJV). The hands of God always lift you up when we are feeling down, and God understands our circumstances.

The love that Jesus has for you above our knowledge of trying to figure out his compassion for us. Sometimes your emotion will try to get the best of you and just step back let God handle the problem. It is imperative you don't ever get to involve with your feelings, and it can lead you to wrong thinking, and direction. The storm can't win, God has your destiny in his hands.

We sometimes are caught in a situation, and the enemy try to make us think you left alone. God, cares too much for us, and will never leave his children in the wilderness. There are times it seems like God not close around, and it feels like you are sinking in your problem. "Call unto me, and I will answer thee, and shew great mighty things, which thou knowest it not" (KJV). God has the answer for every situation going own in your life, and there no one else can ever change the outcome in our life but God. The storm can't win, God has your destiny in his hands.

God is right there all the time even in your weakest moments, and when you don't see a way. God is always making away for you even when the enemy tries to make you feel sad. God will make a river in the desert, and bring you out of that situation you are going through right now.

It is imperative not to confine ourselves from others, and it will allow the enemy to play tricks with your mind. It essential to surround yourself with the church family, love ones, and friends. God will never leave us alone, and he desire to take care us not letting nothing happen to us.

Sometimes you are struggling with the spirit of loneliness is a dangerous life to live filled with no hope, and disappointment.

"Fear thou not; fore I am with thee: be not dismayed; for I am thy God: I will strengthen thee; yea, I will help thee; yea, I will uphold thee with my right hand of my righteousness" (KJV). God does not want us to be frighten, and confused, misunderstood, unhappy.

The God, we are serving wants us to be free, and never feeling down, trusting him every step of the way in our life. The enemy job is to try make the people of God feel alone, rejected, pushed aside, abandon by people. God will bring you out the storm of depression, hardship in your life. The storm can't win, God has your destiny in his hands. Sometimes a sense of loneliness will appear when you in the present of the enemy tries to pull you down.

When we are alone it not the right preparation place for negative and self- critical thoughts to be entertain. It is imperative to understand the enemy first start playing tricks, leading to behavior problems, and being too lonely, making an individual feel no one loves you. "For the Lord will not forsake his people for his great name's sake: because it has pleased the Lord to make you his people" ((KJV). God will not reject us like a man, and sometimes people will not show love but only reject you. The storm can't win, God has your destiny in his hands.

The word of God is a hiding placing in the darkest hour of your storm, and God is waiting with his arms stretch wide open. Sometimes we may feel rejected like David was going through his darkest hour before dawn. "Yea, though I walk through the valley of shadow of death, I will fear no evil: for thou art with me; thy rod and thy staff they comfort me" (k J V). David was praying while going through his storm, and trusting that God was going to bring him out with his mighty hand. The enemy had surrounded David trying to destroy him, and make him give up on God. It is essential to keep your mind on God, and never let the enemy make you feel like you are in a box, and stuck in a corner. David confidence was in God to deliver him from his enemies. The storm can't win, God has your destiny in his hands.

God will never give up on you, and it is imperative to keep our minds focus in the right direction of saying we are not alone. The enemy wants the people of God to have a pity party and feeling down about themselves. The closer you get to God is the safest place for us in the whole wide world, and you will remain happy.

It is imperative to understand that when the enemy tries to shadow you with that spirit of nobody loves you, and it is lonely. You tell the devil storm can't win God has my destiny on his hands. The enemy will come in different forms trying to get you into that state of loneliness and discourage you about God not hearing your cry. God is all seeing, and know everything that goes on in our lives. Jesus had carried all our weakness while on the cross, and God able to ease our pain, loneliness, rejection. The storm can't win, God has your destiny in his hands.

It is essential always to show someone else love, and they do not have to walk alone. Yes, there are times we may feel rejected, and not loved by our love ones or friends Jesus is love. "There is no fear in love; but perfect love castes out fear: because fear had torment" (KJV). It is God will for us to walk in love, and it is important for the children of God not to allow the enemy try to keep creeping in your life. God will never leave you alone. There is no need of us being afraid Jesus on our side. The storm can't win, God has your destiny in his hands.

There are times we spend walking with our friends, and you will not be going in opposite directions. Sometimes your friends will walk in a different direction, and you are not able to listen to their voice. There is no clear

communication while walking alone, and you can't enjoy

their conversation because it is not understood. The daily

walk with Jesus is going to put you in position with God's

will for your life. It is imperative to stay focus on walking

with Jesus in the same direction, and do not get distracted

along the way.

People walking together on the same track field began to

know one another fairly, well by communicating together.

The communication you have with Jesus is entirely

different, and it is more rewarding to have God walking by

our side every day. The time we spend walking with God is

a oneness in the spirit, praying in our secret place.

The connection with God is spending time through

dedicating ourselves in the face of God. There are times in

our life friends walk away, and leave you alone not

understanding the reason why they left us. Life sometimes

has up's, and down people sometimes just in our life for a

season. There is a reason people not meant walk with us all the way on our journey, and it was in God's plan.

God will never fail us and will continue to walk with his children every day and want ever forget you through the storm. "My sheep know my voice, and I know them, and they follow me" (K J V). It is essential to know when God is speaking, and go in the direction he is leading us to go every day. The direction of man is not always the right way, and it may lead us down the wrong path. The ways of the Lord are always correct, and it will never mislead you in the wrong direction. God's ways are always perfect in thy sight, and is precise.

God will wipe away your tears

We are made by the hands of God and blessed to be one of his children. We sometimes will hurt, and cry through our struggles in life that cause us pain. The tears that flow from our little eyes are count by God, and he knows every pain. The tears we are crying in the midnight help bring healing in our life through our afflictions, and trouble.

God has made us so beautifully that he allowed our eyes release tears to remove dirt. God had designed our eyes to see, and make tears when we are hurting, sad, and joyful. When we are sometimes going through a situation, and we began to cry it helps ease the pain, and the burden.is uplifted.

The tears we are crying it releases a healing in our heart, mind, and your body to help bring deliverance. It is imperative to allow the tears to flow and let God move in our life to bring forth a healing. Your tears will sometimes block you from seeing other things clearly example, trying to read your Bible. Sometimes when the Spirit of God is all over you, and you are just thinking about the goodness of Jesus the tears start to flow down your face.

"And David was greatly distress; for the people speak of stoning him, because the souls of all the people was grieved, every man for his son, and for his daughter: David encouraged himself in the Lord his God" (KJV). David cried out to the Lord because of the things he was going through, and suffered pain, and the affliction.

David was not giving up without a fight and was determined to win that battle. David had done what God commanded him to do, and won the battle with great joy. Sometimes we may cry through our struggles in life, and you still have to push, and go on in the name of Jesus. The storm can't win God has your destiny in his hands.

Sometimes you are in bed tossing, and turning, crying, hurting, and you asking God what to do. Lord, what must I do? Sometimes we ask these questions, and sometimes no direct answers right then that moment. God, is still right by your side, and while you are waiting to hear the Lord, speak the direction to follow. You are still waiting on the instruction from God, and your eyes are filled with the tears of joy.

There were times David cried many days and nights unto the Lord, and God had delivered David in the midst his tears. We must do like David still trust God even when things still look impossible. Example, I was told the sight in my left eye was gone, and God restored my eye sight back to me. I had laid in my bed many of nights crying asking God to please do it for me. The tears that were rolling down eyes my cheeks the hurt, and pain going through this situation not understanding the reason. The storm couldn't win, God has your destiny in his hands.

God brought me to the test, and the Lord gave me a testimony through that trial. While my tears were flowing from my eyes every day, and God was working something out for me right then that very moment. There were times my vision got a little cloudy along the way, and that day

God stop by to wipe the tears from my eyes in the storm. The storm can't win, God has your destiny in his hands.

The tears God had dried up with his nail scared hands healed my eye that day, and was able to see again. I had cried out to God, and focusing on my healing, and believing the storm is passing over. Jesus wanted me to trust him, and stop thinking about the problem. I felt the present of the Lord with me in the room that day clearing my vision to see with a new eyesight.

It is imperative for us to wait on the Lord to give us the direction with a clear vision, and seek the wisdom from God goodness always. "Go, and say to Hezekiah, Thus saith the LORD, the God of David thy father, I have heard thy prayer, I have seen thy tears: behold, I will add unto thy days fifteen years" (KJV). Hezekiah was sick near death struck him down, and a prophet name Isaiah was sent by God to tell Hezekiah to get his house in order.

The word of God touched his life that very moment, and Hezekiah turned his face to the wall crying out to the Lord. The tears were flowing from Hezekiah's eyes God heard his prayers and healed his body adding fifteen more years to his life. It is imperative to have a pure heart before God and serve him with joy.

Sometimes we get a little worried along the way and wondering which way to turn. Is your vision foggy today? God able to clear our sight to see a better view, and find the right road to follow in life. Sometimes life like a tree with many branches connected to it, and some branches are bearing up well and spreading out in different directions. It is imperative to understand "in life" we sometimes need to make the decision about different things that may adapt to our lifestyle.

It is essential not never to move too fast, and make a huge mistake, and just take your time to thinks it out. God is always the head of our life, and the first important step is to acknowledge God before making any plans. "I waited patiently for the LORD; and he inclined unto me, and heard my cry" (KJV). David had no doubt in his mind God was going to come to his rescue, and there nothing too hard for the Lord. Even in the midst our tears it is a little hard to see our way in the storm, and waiting on God is the right way. The storm can't win, God has your destiny in his hands.

There are times we may cry, and weeping in tears for the family member that is sick needing a healing in their body. It is imperative to keep on praying because God sees every hurt and sincere pray that goes before the Lord day and night. We can't give up praying because you have not seen a change in that person life yet. It is essential to keep right on praying for days, weeks, months or a year. God is always listening to us, and see the need before we bow down to pray every day. "The effectual fervent prayer of a righteous man availeth" (KJV). God able to see every tear drop and every heart felt prayer from our lips. The storm comes to try to distract you from the plan of God.

Sometimes our eyes may get a little misty through the tears rolling down our face, and trying to understand right away. The enemy seeks to distract to get your mind off the will of God. It is imperative to keep our minds on Jesus and wipe the tears continue to pray God holds the answer to your problem. God will come to your rescue, and deliver out of the storm.

Example, you down on the ground crying, and you cut your knee it is bleeding wipe it off put a bandage on it keep on going. We can't continue laying there bleeding, tears flowing, and you not able to put a bandage on the cut spot. We must wipe our tears and get a clear vision to access the situation, and allow God to direct our path. The storm can't win, God has your destiny in his hands.

Sometimes we are going through storms, and it will bring tears to your eyes just hold on a little while the healing process to take place in your life. It is hard sometimes to come out the confront zone into a rough spot in life. God will deliver you through sickness and your faith level will increase while waiting on God for your deliverance. It is essential to keep our eyes on God and don't give up cause a change will come in your life. "Weeping may endure for a night, but joy will cometh in the morning" (KJV). We don't know how long that morning is early, midday or night, and God is always on time.

God able heal you through your tears, heartache, troubles, afflictions, and a blessing will come out of your trials. Yes, through all the tears flowing, and staying up at nights God is right by your side. God know everything about us right from our head to our toes, and it is blessing that only God knows. Yes, God knows how many times you had cried during the day, and when you stop weeping. The storm can't win, God has your destiny in his hands.

"I will cry unto God most high; unto God that perform all things for me" (KJV). Every child of God has a distinctive cry, and the sound only Jesus knows when to answer us. The sound of your cry Jesus already knows your need, and he will come to see about us. David had cried out unto God in the midst his enemies, and God had stepped in to save him from destruction.

We serve a God that will come and see about us in the midst our storm and wipe the tears away. "They that sow in tears shall reap a harvest" (KJV). Example, a farmer will plant a seed in the ground, and it will soon produce a harvest. Our praying, release tears, and faithfulness are offered up unto God a river of blessings getting ready to overtake you. The storm can't win, God has your destiny in his hands.

When we are crying, it signifies something wrong, and your heart were broken. The purpose of tears is to help cleanse us from the things broken that try to block our spiritual, intellectual, and physical health and healthy lifestyle. The tears are running from your eyes represented as pain, and positioning yourselves for a change to take place in life.

Your situation may have started out bad, and God can step in bring good out of the storm. It is imperative to understand God has equipped us to endure the pain and the tears that try to interrupt our life. You may think your life is hanging on the edge during the storm. Even through your weeping God see the hurt, and God can erase all your bad days, and all your good days will outweigh more than you can imagine in your life. The storm can't win, God has your destiny in his hands.

The hands of the Master are shaping you into a beautiful piece designed vessel from the potter's wheel. God is all knowing where everyone supposed to fit in on the earth. The tear drops that flows from your eyes, and God knows the expressing, and out the soul of every woman, and man the pain is just for a season in the storm. "Thou tellest my wondering: put my tears into thy bottle: are they not in thy book?" (KJV). God knows every day we had cried for sorrow, pain, stress, struggles, heartache, and hardship. Every one of your tear drops is kept in the bottle, and recorded in God's book.

We will never be able to count the water that flows from our eyes, and you will not always remember the reason for crying in the storm. The struggle, affliction, and only God will remember those days, and he will count the tears we cried. Sometimes our heart is hurting because of pain or trouble, sickness, disappointment, and weighted down by the cares of the world. The tears will flow from the eyes, and your broken heart and it smashed into thousands of pieces. The storm that tried to invade your home, job, sickness, finances, family, mentally, and physically. The storm can't win, God has your destiny in his hands.

The tears we had cried God know what cause the problem in your life in the storm. Do you remember all the tears you cried? No, we will never remember all the days, and nights you sat up weeping unto the Lord. It is awesome God remembers and record them all in a book, and keeps them in a bottle for us in heaven. I am so happy no one able to go in take none our tears out of the bottle or the book recorded by God. The tears we cry every day is not always grief, pain, heartache, loneliness, sadness in life.

We are weeping sometimes cause you happy about an exciting life event, example a birth of a child. The time is never too far spent expressing the tears, and laughter about some joyful occasion celebrated. "A time to weep, and a

time laugh, and a time to mourn, and time to dance" (KJV).
It is amazing how God can allow us to laugh, and cry at the
same time. A life filled with laughter, tears, pain, and
behind every sob eye there is a story to tell. Your eyes
filled with tears wiped with a napkin, and absorb in the
paper towel throw away. The storm can't win, God has
your destiny in his hands.

Your tears drop had failed on the desktop, and Jesus came
to put all my tears in a bottle none disappeared. "The eyes
of the Lord are on the righteous, and his ears open to their
cry" (KJV). Sometimes we will pray alone in a quiet place,
bedroom, bathroom, shower, and don't let anyone see us
cry. God able to see all your tears when love ones and
friends can't see our tears. Crying is a part of life, and God
had designed it for a purpose and a plan in our life. The
storm that almost took you out without warning, and God
has his arms around us. The storm can't win, God has your
destiny in his hands.

The power to praise God

The praises we have offer unto God gives us a great honor to walk in the present of the Mighty King Jesus. Every day is a blessing to bow before God, and I thank the Lord for all the beautiful things he has done for me. The storms that were roaring in my life God spoke and the turmoil shifted into the outer darkness never to come again. God will send his remarkable power to bring forth deliverance for us. Sometimes we are surrounded by different problems in life, and the enemy will try to stop your blessings.

The devil will try to bring stress in your life to stop you from praising God, and the wants to bound you up. It is imperative to keep a praise on the inside of your spirit man to help push you to a breakthrough. Our deliverance is in the praise, and you must push yourself to get into the atmosphere of praise and worshipping God. The enemy

will try to detract you from God and get you out of the will
of God.

One of the biggest tricks the enemy will use try to make
you think God does not love you enough to come and see
about us in the midst your storm. It does not matter what
the situation looks like in your life, and it is essential to
keep pressing and praising your way through the situations.
You should remember there is a reason the Lord want you
to continue praise his name, and God has a plan for our life.

Our Heavenly Father is working out some things in your
favor, and even you can't trace the God's hand prints
working on your case. The Lord is already fixing
somethings in your life behind the scene. We will sometime
go through a tiny problem, and the enemy will try to blow
it up make it bigger than it appears. "When the enemy shall
come in like a flood, the spirit of the Lord shall lift up a
standard against him" (KJV). When we, lift our voices like

a trumpet it will make the devil flee with the praises of God going forth in the atmosphere.

The word of God and the praises from our lips will break down the strongholds of the enemy. The enemy can't stand the blessings of God, and calling on Jesus name has power. "Resist the devil he will flee from you" (KJV). It is essential to withstand, and not to give into the temptation or tricks of the enemy.

The word of God is our valuable weapon to tearing down all wick devices of the devil. Prayer and Praises of God is a powerful tool to help release your blessings. "Put on the whole armour of God, that ye maybe able to stand against the wiles of the devil" (KJV). There are some attacks the enemy try to throw out against you, and will try to defeat you in the storm. The storm can't win, God has your destiny on his hands.

The power of praise will allow you to help defeat the enemy no matter what your struggles you are facing today. Example, the devil will try to make you lose your job for no reason just because they do not like the way you look, and dress. "For we wrestle not against flesh and blood, but against the principalities, against powers, against rulers of the darkness of this world, against spiritual wickedness in high places" (KJV). These are attacks the enemy try to send out to stop you from being blessed by God.

God praises release from your mouth will bring forth deliverance, and when it looks like you are trap all alone. The blessings of God will liberate our breakthrough, and the Glory of the Lord will rain down upon your life. When the Spirit of Jesus Christ will rain down on you, and your cup began to fill back up with the blessings. It is important to see the Glory of God reveal in the land through praising the name of the Lord release changes in our school, homes, jobs, churches, community, and bring healing for us.

God is always in control of our life every day, and the Lord desires the praises of his people. Jesus has given us the power, and the authority to stop the plan of the enemy with our praise, through the word. There is power through praises, and keeping our minds focus on God while offering up our praises for the victory. God gave Jehoshaphat, and his people the victory through praises and focusing on the Lord. The storm can't win, God your destiny in his hands.

God, I will trust you

God already know the storm that will appear in our life, and the Lord able to stop the plan of the enemy. There is a reason the causes the turmoil to happen in our lives, and God has the authority to make it cease. Our faith will sometimes tried, and God will build us up to be strong through your trails in life.

God has already given his people the victory through the blood of Jesus, and there nothing able to shake your faith. It is imperative never to get afraid of the turmoil that may be surrounding you. "For in the time of trouble he shall hide me in his pavilion: in the secret of his tabernacle shall he hide me; he shall set me up upon a rock" (KJV). David had faith to believe, and trust God through all the persecution from his enemies, and David believe the Lord will take care of him in the storm.

God is the only way out of your situation to trust, and obey the word of Lord. "Ye are of God little children, and have overcome them: because greater is he that is in you, than he that is in the world" (KJV). Jesus live on the inside of us there should not be any fear of nothing going on around us every day, and the hands of the Lord is upon your life. God will always protect you with his mighty hands, and the angels of Lord camp in front, back, each side of us.

The blood of Jesus will cover us in the midst the enemy to stand still, and trust God in the storm. The hands of God will sustain you in the present of the turmoil to keep the faith and believe the Lord for the victory. Sometimes the storm will try to take your eyes off Jesus and get you afraid of the wind that is blowing in your life.

God want us to trust, and don't give up regardless how the situations may look right now. God will never leave us alone in the midst the serious battle going around you, and we should never get alarmed just keep our trust in the Lord. The hands of the Lord were on me when going through an operation, and the enemy tried to bring fear to my heart three days before the surgery.

God said I am a doctor even in your hospital room, and the chief surgeon on staff in that room with you so there is no need of being afraid. My heart was filled with joy just to hear the voice God of speaking to me letting me know to trust him in the midst the storm. The Spirit of the Lord lifted me up in a peaceful atmosphere. I believe God spoken words in my life to trust him, and don't give up. It is essential to give all your troubles, fears, heartache to the Lord, and allow Jesus to release peace in your life. "Casting all of your cares upon him; for he careth for you" (KJV). God is concerned about us, and every little thing that goes on in our life. The problems we are facing Jesus wants us to ask him to handle it, and just trust him with the matter.

Trusting God is an essential part of our everyday life, and taking him at his word. There are some things people keep their confidence in today, and the material things in life can fail you, and God will never decline you. It is hard to put your faith in some friend or family member because sometimes they may not even workout all the time. God is worthy, and the Lord can be trusted all the time does not matter "about the type of problem" you may be encounter in life.

We can get on our knees, and tell God anything nothing will get repeated back us. Jesus will never break his actual relationship with you, and turn his back on his children like other people may do us. God is trustworthy to his people and will stick with you through every problem, and the situation in life. Daniel trusted God, even when going throw in the lion's den to be eaten up.

The evil men went to King Darius, and ask him to make agreed that no man prays to God for thirty days. The King already knew that Daniel was not going to stop praying, and he decided to go ahead put him in the Lion's Den to see how much did Daniel trusted his God.

King Darius was sure in his heart that Daniel could not be spared in the midst the Lions, and would be eaten alive by the Loins before the next morning. It was surprising to the King that Daniel survived being in the den with all those big hungry Lions walking around. The Lion's mouth was closed by the hands of the Lord on the behalf of Daniel that day.

"Daniel was taking up out of the den no matter of hurt was found upon him, because he believed in his God' (KJV). Daniel had trusted God with his life in the midst the loins, and he knew God was going to bring him through the test. Have you ever been to a point in your life you felt you were in a lion's den? You had love ones and friends staying by watching you saying what you are going to do now? While you are in the midst the storm, and you are trusting God to bring you out. The storm can't win, God has your destiny in his hands.

"My God had sent his angel, and shut the loins' mouths, that they have not hurt me: forasmuch as before him innocency was found in me; and also before thee, O King have I done no hurt" (KJV). Daniel was not worried about being harmed in the midst the lions and he came out victorious. The enemy has tried to stop you along the way and was seeking to hinder your job, finances, family, healing. The storm can't win, God your destiny in his hands.

Sometimes in life, it may feel like you are in a loin den, and the enemy will desire to see the people fall. It is imperative we put all of our trust in God regardless the type of situations that may arise in your life. "Behold God is my salvation; I will trust, and not be afraid: for the lord JEHOVAH is strength and my song; he also is become my salvation" (KJV). It is imperative to trust, and to know God is for you, and able to deliver you. The hands of God able to take care of us, and just take God at his word trust the Lord in all his ways.

Trust means to have complete confidence in God, and not wavering with unbelief. A man will sometimes put their faith in houses, cars, land, silver, and gold these worldly goods can fade away out of your life. The love, trust in God will forever stand in our life even when man and woman will sometimes walk out of your life. It is imperative to understand the trust we can put in Jesus never gets old or shift to another side.

A man or woman can open a book or close it, and God will never close an invitation to come into your life. Yes, it is good to trust your family, and friends at a certain extent in our life. "It better to trust in the Lord than put confidence in man" (KJV). We can totally depend on God's word and faithful to his promises concerning us.

The nature side of a human may not always keep their word, and they may fail to meet their obligation in life. God is always on time never forget any of his appointments, and we can trust God. Sometimes life can be confusing to some people, and they do not know how to trust God in their heart.

Sometimes life will take you on a fast track, and will try cause you to lose your footage when you don't have God on board. The changes in life are almost like a road coaster you travel through a lot of curves, and it is hard to focus on your journey. You will sometimes feel stress and exhausted from being on your trip. The storm can't win, God has your destiny in his hands.

There is sometimes exertion, and infirmity may try to destroy your life with financial struggles, and things may not go as plan. Who can I trust to help me? "The LORD also will be a refuge for the oppressed, a refuge in times of trouble" (KJV). We have total trusted our assurances in God and know Jesus will take care of us all times in life. Sometimes the enemy will try to make us lose our hope in the word of God.

We must continue to stand confident in the Lord and do not get discouraged about the things going around us in the world. "Every word of God is pure: he is a shield unto them that put their trust in him" (KJV). It is imperative to understand the promises of Jesus is right, and he will take care of his people that believe.

We must trust God at his word, and never doubt it just stand firm to see the hands of the Lord work in our life. There were some things you may face in your life, and God already knew the test before it appeared in your life. The situation you have approached another stage in your life, and God had quickened your Spirit to trust him with the issues.

You must take your eyes off the problem while putting our focus and trust in God. "Now the God of hope fill you with all joy and peace in believing, that ye may abound in hope, through the power of the Holy Ghost" (KJV). Our sensitivity is overwhelmed with the peace of God, and continue to trust in the Lord.

PART- SIX

___

We all faces challenges

There are challenges we face every day of our live and sometimes uphill situations. Sometimes life gets a little complicated for people to try to master alone, and they do not understand the reason behind the storms. It is imperative for us to grasp in our mind that it is a part of life, and God able to handle your problems that appear in your life. There are things we must adapt daily, and it is sometimes personal, homes, money, job. It is imperative to understand there is no need to get frightened and walk away from the problems, and God is bigger than your issues.

Walking away from the challenges is not going to solve the situation, and it will only delay it. It essential not to get upset about your problem, and try not to make the wrong choice. There is a reason for sitting down and thinking things out in the proper perspective to avoid destruction to take place in your life. It is Important to understand that making the right decisions in life can save you from regret, heartache, and pain. The best way to handle our challenges in life is to relax, and think things out clearly before saying this is the right answer today.

You must embrace life one day at a time, and sometimes it is not always the way you want things to be in your life. There are some people you may talk to every day, and they may not have the same ideas and may not be on the same level. We are not going to agree on the same things all the time in life, and yet we sometimes disagree but still have to come to a decision.

We are adults living every day facing challenges in the world, and it imperative to understand no one can alter someone mind. Sometimes it is good to have challenges, and it will help make you mature person in life the way God wants us. "My brothers count it joy when you fall into diver temptations" (KJV). When there is a challenge in your life, and you got to focus on God believing that he will fill you with joy.

There will be some situation that comes in your life to make you, and not to break you down. It is imperative not to let the problem take control of you, and learn to handle the challenges under pressure with wisdom. There is always a starting point to things in the right direction without angry taking control in your life.

It is imperative not to step out of bound, and take things out on the co-workers, family, and friends. "There is no temptation that taken you but such as is common to man but God is faithful, who will not suffer you to be tempted above that that ye are able, but will with the temptation also make a way to escape, that may be able to bear it" (KJV).

There are situations in life that may try to come press you

down, and God is always there to bring you through your

storm.

We have to stay on course, and you can't get sidetrack

about things that are going on around you every day. God

able to give you peace in the midst your storm, and it does

not matter where you may be in the world God is right

there by your side. The first thing the enemy will try to

attack is your mind, and bring confusion with wrong

messages that need to be deleted by the blood of Jesus.

"The thief cometh not, but fore to steal, and to kill and to

destroy: I am come that they might have life, and that they

might have it more abundantly" (KJV).

Sometimes through struggles, the enemy will try to break

your peace, and cause angry, frustration, disappointment to

take place in your life. You will accomplish the task that

God sits before us, and you don't ever have to be afraid to talk to the Lord. You may have a challenge with a big test that seems to be a little complicated to your eyes, and the enemy tried to make you think it was too much to absorb in your mind. The word of God came to me "I can do all things through Christ which strengthen me" (KJV).

Example, sometimes you are facing a big challenge taking an extended test, and God brought you through to pass it with an A. We have to give all the Glory, and praises unto God cause "without the Lord" you could not complete the assignment. The mission that day was accomplished, and God gave you the victory to overcome the challenge.

Jesus will teach you through any life challenge there no need of being afraid, and God will bring you through every time. There are times in everyone life people go through heartache, pain, and still believing God will help them through the storm. The storm can't win, God has your destiny in his hands.

We know that Jesus is never late, and always on time in the midst the challenging moments in our life. There are times you look for your friends or family to help you, and there is no one to come to your rescue. God will never forget about you, and he knows every need in your home to take care of the situations in your life.

God has all the power in his hands, and the problem is never too heavy for the Master to carry on his shoulder. Sometimes you may feel like there is a big red sea in your life, and you are not able to cross to the other side. The storm can't win, God has your destiny in his hands.

Finding your purpose

Sometimes people don't use the correct collected thoughts and setting original and spiritual goals in life. It is imperative to make all your plans, and spiritually lead by God to point you in the right direction, and your future is serious matter. It is always good to go, and seek the Lord to ask him to show you the right way in life. It is important to listen, and clearly here the voice of the Lord, and we don't want to make the biggest mistake of our life by not following God instructions.

There are so many blessing God has stored in our life to use, and go forth to do God's will at the appropriate time. The gifts God has placed in our life should be used to help fulfill our purpose in life, and not waste it doing nothing every day. God has a purpose for our life try to reach the destination, and live a rewarding career and fulfill our dreams.

There was a man in the Bible hide his talent "And I was afraid, and went and hid thy talent in the earth: lo, there thou hast that is thine" (KJV). God had blessed the man with special gifts, and he was afraid to use it for the Glory

of God. Example, sometimes people are gifted to build

houses, and will not get a job as a carpenter. We should ask

God to give us the faith to walk in our gifts, and the calling

we are ordain.

There are ways to set your goals in life, and it is

imperative not to back up from your purpose in life. We

may have to take our time, and search out the plan first find

out the correct road to take without failing your vision to

pursue your dreams. It is essential to understand we made

by the precious hands of God.

"I will praise thee; for I am fearfully and wonderfully

made: marvelous are thy works; and that my soul knoweth

right well" (KJV). The hands of God that created us already

knew our future, and give us the gift to walk in healthy

place. The will of God needs fulfilling in every part of our

life to reach the plans that will benefit us. It is imperative to maintain the goals that agree with our spiritual convictions. It is essential not to set goals that go against the will of God for your life, and it will cause you to lose your strength, hope, mentally, peace, and joy. God had created us to commune with him, and others to have a fulfill life on the earth must show a balance. The purpose is peerless and extraordinary, and the individual maybe you, and you can help another person.

What is God's purpose for your life? It is imperative to pursue your calling to reach your destiny in life. There is a plan for everyone, and today it does not matter how large the project maybe it just need to reach your destination to fulfill your dreams. It is essential to be on the right road, and you do not have to turn around again to start over. A deep calling to your purpose indicates more than a task to perform in your life.

It does not matter the type of work we are doing

everyday life. The primary purpose in our life is to follow

the plan God has for us, and knowing the right path to

follow to your destination. Life is so much rewarding when

knowing where you are heading in the right direction. We

have a better inner peace living on the inside of our heart,

and knowing this is the right place for us.

It is imperative to be a goal- oriented person knowing

your position, and going forth in your calling that is the

purpose for your life. The will of God already set up for

you to stand, and believe in your purpose. The love God

has for us more precious than any diamond in a jewelry

store downtown.

It is essential walking, talking, and you have a spiritual

relationship with God to find your purpose in life. It is

imperative to learn, and understand the voice of God to

continue communicating with the Lord every day. It is

essential not to get slack talking to God, and knowing your purpose to do the will of God. I know there are some of us wonder how to pursue our purpose in life? Life can sometime be a complicated path to follow without Jesus in your corner. It is imperative not spend a lot of time thinking on your own without consulting first God. Our life is designed for plans, and directions to follow to gain a successful life for the Glory of God.

You may have experienced a sudden blow like bumping into a brick wall. It is imperative let nothing stop you from reaching your destiny. There is always a situation that may arise in your life, and giving up is not an option. The storm can't win God has your destiny in his hands. It is imperative to follow the directions of God to lead and guide you through all truth.

It will bring great pleasure in your life when finding the purpose to fulfill your dreams, and visions. The plans of

God will fall into place for you through faith, and knowing your purpose God had already designed for you to walk in life. The storm can't win, God has your destiny in his hands.

We can't continue to look at the problems going on around you and miss your purpose in God. "I press toward the mark for the prize of the high calling of God in Christ Jesus" (KJV). The enemy will try lurking out, and try to pull you back and try to stop you from going forth in God. Sometimes in your life may look a little confusing, and you do not understand the right path to follow.

You can't continue to stand in the dark, and not knowing what to do next, and to find your purpose in life. "Thy word is the lamp unto my feet, and a light unto my path" (KJV). It is essential to follow the word of God, and it is a bright light that never goes dim. The road we supposed to be traveling is in the plans of God and follow daily.

Your purpose is directing it in the divine order that according the God's plans. "Samuel grew up, and the Lord was with him, and did let none of his words fall to the ground" (KJV). God already had a plan for Samuel life to be a prophet for Israel. Samuel kept hearing the voice of the Lord speaking to him while he was laying down sleep, and he got up asking Eli who was calling him in the middle of the night.

After the third call, Eli told Samuel to say here am I Lord, and he follows the direction that was given to do that hour. God already had a plan for Samuel life to become a prophet for Israel. It was imperative that Samuel knew the purpose God had for him to follow, and carrying it out in the divine order.

God had a major role for Samuel to grasp in give an account to the task. Do you know God's will for your life today? It is God will for us to know his plans for our life, and follow the ways of the Lord.   Sometimes people do not understand the will of God for their life. The plans God has for our life is necessary, and he desire us to walk in that place with purpose.

"Listen, O isle, unto me; and hearken, ye people from far; The Lord called me from the womb; from the bowls of my mother hath he made mention of my name" (KJV). It is already mention by the hands of God our purpose before we were birth from our mother womb. We are faced with struggles every day there still a plan in your life. It is imperative to understand we wonderfully created by God's hands.

God is calling for you to do something right now, and the enemy is trying to stop your destiny. It is imperative to stay focus in the midst of the storm and find a resting place with God. "Before I formed you in the belly I knew thee; before thou camest forth out of the womb I sanctified thee, and I ordain thee a prophet unto the nations" (KJV). The hands of God were already on Jeremiah before he came out of his mother womb a plan was ready in place for his life be a prophet.

There are things we may not understand while growing up in the stages of life. We know that God allows us to be born on the earth, and the birth from our mother womb. During the process, we are going through our stages in life, and you were trying to find your purpose in life. We are continuing trying to find what is missing in our daily route beside working, home, raising children, and paying bills. Have you experienced there must be more to life than just this same pattern in life, and something is missing?

"For I know the thoughts that I think toward you saith the Lord, thoughts of peace, and not of evil, to give you expected end" (KJV). It is God desire to prosper you, and no wise bring anyone harm to you only to prosper us. It is imperative for us to have a close relationship with God, and

to learn the real living King. We are God's disciples, and

you should follow Jesus every step of the way, and not lean

not to the left or right. It is essential to have the Holy Spirit

living on the inside of us which will lead us into all truth.

"Howbeit when he, the Spirit of truth.is come he will

guide you into all truth; for he shall not speak of himself;

but whatsoever he shall hear; that shall he speak: and he

will show you things to come" (KJV). God will teach, and

guide you to follow your purpose to reach our destiny. The

full expectation that is ordained by God, and he already has

a blessing plan for us.

It is essential to walk into your destiny that God purposes

for you, and it is imperative to keep the faith on the

journey. Sometimes a person may not find their aspiration

because they are not following God's commands, and they

are not being obedient to the will of God. It is important to seek the face of the Lord and get the directions that God

has a plan for you. God able take you through the storm

and give you the divine revelation for your life. Sometimes

things may seem out of control, and no end to the drama in

your life. The storm can't win, God has your destiny in his

hands.

There must be divine order to connect to the will of God

for the journey you must take with no turning back, and

pressing on. The nights may be far spent with darkness all

around you and trying to find your way out of the storm.

God do not want us to be afraid, and the enemy desire to try

to block the connection for your life. "If God be for you

who can be against you" (KJV). God is always on your side

it does not matter about no one else opinion. The storm

can't win, God has your destiny in his hands.

God is the one that lives inside, and give us the air to

breath God will grant us the best life, and serve him to the fullness for his Glory. Do we know our purpose here on the earth? God did not just put us here to take up space, and do nothing every day with our lives. First, it is imperative to know your purpose for God to show us his plan to follow, and to do his will on the earth. There will always be some disappointment, and the enemy will try to wave some distraction in your face strive to stop your progress in God.

The enemy will continue trying setting roadblocks in the way to keep you from reaching your destiny. "According to the grace of God which is given unto me, as a wise master builder, I have laid the foundation, and another buildeth thereon" (KJV). God have laid the foundation for us to follow, and build on it to fulfill the purpose with our hands. It is imperative we do not let another man or woman take the place that belongs to us and lose out on your blessing.

God is the chief Master Builder in our life, and it is essential to worship the King, Lord of Lord, the ruler of everything in the universe. Sometimes things that might

seem right to a man, and it is not the plan of God. "In all

thy ways acknowledge him, and he shall direct thy path"

(KJV). We must trust the Lord and follow the

commandments that he given to us, and reach our

destinations in life. It is imperative to finding your purpose

is seeking the face of God, and staying motivated, and

never give up on your dreams. It is imperative to

understand how to pursue your purpose, and God will show

you the plan for your life. The storm can't win God has

your destiny in his hands.

PART- SEVEN

The powerful hands of God that brought me out

The anointing and the power of God made me see he can

do anything except but fail. It did not matter about how I

tried to stop the pain, struggles, and the fear. God, step right in my life and made the storm surrender to his voice. Jesus "Then he arose, and rebuke the wind and the sea, and there was a great calm" (KJV). I had to learn to move back and let God handle my problems that were trying to destroy me.

The mighty hands of God moved upon my life, and Jesus turned my midnight into day. I felt the power of God delivering me from the storm and placing my feet on a solid rock. God have been so glad to me, and even times I could not see it all right before me. "Oh, taste and see that Lord is good" (KJV). I had begun to see the goodness of the Lord resting upon my life and could not understand it all at a young age.

The blessing of the Lord upon my life and he brought me out of the storm. I am thankful even on today for God choosing to bring me out with his loving hands. God could have let me stay in that situation longer, and let me try to handle the problems. God already knew it was impossible for me to do it, and God step right in, and pulled me out.

Example, just like a Captain of a ship following the compass to give the right direction to their destiny. It was God's hands that stopped the plans of the enemy and kept me during the storm. God wants us to see the power that is in the palm of his hands, and Jesus holds our future. I saw the blessing of the Lord, and there was no greater power than Jesus. The storm can't win, God has your destiny in his hands.

God has your destiny

Sometimes people will get impatient, and tried on a long journey. Jesus said, "Call unto me I will answer thee, and shew thee great and mighty things, which thou knowest not" (KJV). You must call on Jesus, and learn of his ways the Lord will take care if you. God wants us to communicate with him, and the Lord will tell you things that world can't see, nor do in your life. You have too still a way by yourself, and you talk to God sometimes in the midnight hours. It is essential to seek the face of God even during your hard times, and learning to communicate in Lord present with joy.

It is imperative to talk with God and listen to to find the right instruction for your destiny. The communication times we are spending with God essential, and the sense of knowing the Lord is in the room with you. I began to call on Jesus every time even before trouble seems to arise in my life, and you are seeking answers to your problem.

God will come to your rescue every time, and it doesn't matter what time day or night. When you feel like your back up against the wall, you just call on the name of Jesus, and God will come to help you. Jesus began to show me the way to my destiny, and God will never let your hands slip out of his hands. The storm can't win, God has your destiny in his hands.

You are safe in the hands of the God, and everything is going to come out alright in your life. It is imperative to be in the right hands, and God is the best place anyone wants to be every day walking along life journey. Sometimes, along the way your friends will try to show you a different direction to go in life, and it may not always be the right way. Life will sometime get a little twisted, and you will try to find a good place, and you what peace in the midst the storm.

"For I the Lord thy God will hold Thy right hand; saying unto the fear not; I will help you" (KJV). It is essential to allow God in your life, and the Lord will always head us in the right direction. Sometimes it is not easy trying to find the right person while walking on the road, and looking for a friend. "Teach me thy way O Lord; I will walk to thy truth: unite my heart to fear thy name" (KJV). It is essential to allow God to instruct us his ways, and don't try to learn on your own. It is impossible to know the right direction without being in the face of God, and inform of his marvelous hands. The storm can't win, God has your destiny in his hands.

"For my thoughts are not your thoughts, neither are ways are my ways, saith the Lord" (KJV). The techniques God uses is not the same way we may think it should be in our life. Example, God speak to you about driving to New York head North You thought it was all the right turns, and following the right road to get your destination. During the travel, you made a wrong turn, and you felt it was the right road   It is imperative to listen to the voice of God and follow the right spiritual direction to get in the correct place with the Lord. Jesus is merciful and it is essential for us to follow the Lord all the time, and God will bring you out with a powerful hand.

It is imperative we know the right directions to follow on this journey "The Lord thy God may shew us the way, wherein we may walk, and the things we may do" (KJV). We have to communicate with God to ask him for the divine instructions to go and to complete our assignments which are required by Lord. Everything we do is related to form of guidance in life that needed along the way. God wants us to have the right understanding, and to live in the proper atmosphere filled with peace.

God is concern about everything we do on the earth large or small agenda in life. When we wake up in the morning, and we should always ask the Lord to show us the way to take on today. Every day we wake up is a brand new, and our directions are made different from yesterday. A new day is a refreshing of something better to happen another journey, and asking God to show us the way.

The ways of the Lord will lead us to the path filled with joy, peace, and understanding that in his present is love.

Sometimes people will ask others to help with a certain situation in their life, and it may cause a bigger mess. It is imperative to understand that there are tricks the devil try to play with your mind, and the enemy will make you think your right.

There is a higher level above man or woman thinking, and trying to find the right directions. There is one thing we must understand, and we must seek the Lord's face everything you desire to do in life. Example, God will speak and warn you to wait and to don't move. When you try to fix the problem on yours on the job, turns into a big mess. It is important to ask God, and we should never get out of the will of the Lord.

There are sometimes problems that may occur in our life and you do not fully understand the direction to take in the matter for it to be resolved. "But they that wait upon the Lord shall renew their strength; they shall mountain up with wing as eagles; they shall run and not be weary; and they shall walk and not faint" KJV). The way sometimes will get a little rough along the way, and you will need God to show you the right direction to follow. The finish line is just a few inches away to receiving the victory, and you get tried almost lose your footage. The storm can't win, God has your destiny in his hands.

We have to remember to ask God for help during your troubled moment to overcome the storm ahead in your life. "I will lift my eyes unto the hills, from whence cometh my help" (KJV). We have to trust the Lord for all of our help, and protection comes from God the maker of heaven and earth. God will hear our cry, and always be there to answer our call in the midst every battle in life. It is imperative to wait, and never try go before God receiving his instruction to take concerning the matter.

The simple things in life God will care about us even down to a string of hair on our head. God have not forgotten about you during your struggles, pain, and all your life painful experiences. It essential to understand God has never lost a case in the ring or the outer court with the enemy. Ask yourself "is there anything too hard for God" (KJV). No there is not one thing to complicated for God, and the Lord will show up, and win every battle for you. The storm can' t win, God has your destiny in his hands.

Walk in your destiny

Sometimes, you will feel a little exhausted, and wondering about your destination point, you must travel. Are we there yet? We will find ourselves asking this question many times, and never finding the answer we are looking for the present moment. Sometimes we are walking, and talking searching to find the right solutions to reach our destiny. Sometimes life seems it is a little tough on your journey, and you just have to keep your heads up don't give up. It does not matter the type of problems you are facing in the storm just maintain the faith in God to bring you through every test.

You will put your faith in God, and don't get exhausted along the way to the place called destiny. You know faith is something we can't see with the nature eyes, and just having the sure confidence, it will come too past. "Now faith is the substance of things hope for, the evidence of things not seen" (KJV). God will bring you to that place called there, and keep you in perfect peace. It is imperative to believe in your heart, and God able to shift you into that location called destiny.

God able to take authority, and put into action just one spoken word is adequate to change your life in a second. Sometimes it will look like the wind may get a little rough during the midnight hours, and God will make the storm cease in the night. God will not let you fall along the way to your destination.

There are two things you can't conquer in the same room that fear, and faith in your heart and mind. The heart has to choose between fear or faith, and some will only fall into the category of fear because it can block your faith if your mind is not in the right position to receive the blessing. It is essential to have the correct mindset to walk into your destiny.

It is imperative to receive the gift called faith to push out the fear that tries to penetrate the heart. In world, today sometimes life filled with fear will try to creep in unaware in the heart. "For God hath not given us the spirit of fear; but of power, and of love, and of a sound mind" (KJV). There is one sure thing God in control of your destiny, and it is the place called there in our life. The storm can't win, God has your destiny in his hands.

It is imperative to understand there is a place called there, and God desires for you to get into that position today. God will speak, and let you know to get ready to walk into your season. It is a place that God has promised to take care of us during your weakest moment, and it seems like there is no hope. God will always do what he said, and the Lord is never slow, and the King of Glory will take care of you. God is waiting, and listening for your prayers, and ready to move on your behalf today. The storm can't win, God has your destiny in his hands.

God will continue to provide for you in the place called there no matter what the situation maybe in your life. It is essential to understand the Lord loves us and wants us to be happy. The love God has for us far above anyone can ask or think in their life. God was never confined by no man on this earth the King of Glory transcends his will to be done. It is imperative to understand our time frame is not like God's not even three seconds, and to you it will feel three days. God have already got things in his control, and working it out for your good. The storm can't win, God has your destiny in his hands.

"And they said him, we have here but five loaves and two fishes" (KJV). Jesus took the two fishes and the five loaves of bread feed 5,000 people on that day. God wanted to show the people he is the Great I Am, one can take care of them in that place, and meet their needs. God will provide for you, and just trust the Lord.

God had worked signs, and wonders before the people, and there was healing, spiritual feeding of the word, and the nature food given to feed the people. God had made provision for his people in the place to feed them that very hour. God will always make a way for us, and the enemy will try to make you feel like there is no hope. We serve a God of provision for us today, and not a division. I believe the people had faith, and knew the Lord was going to take care them, and family. "But my God shall supply all your needs according to his riches in glory by Christ Jesus" (KJV). We should not worry about anything because Jesus is a great provider for us.

It is imperative just trust the word of God, and never get side track about our provision. Jesus had taken care of the birds, and the grass on the earth and God able to provide for his people as well. God's anointing power was flowing among the people to see the miracle perform. The children of God had nothing to eat, and the Lord took the two fish, five loaves of bread placed in a basket turn out to feed five thousand people.

They have never seen these miracles happen before, and the power of God reveal it in their present. It is God's desire for us to receive the blessing from his hands, and manifest his power for his Glory. Why some people will never get to the place call "there" now? It is because the individual does not have enough faith in God to put the situation in the Master's hands. You are now in the midst the storm in your life, and your back is up against the wall trying to find your way out. "Now faith is the substance of things hoped for evidence of things not seen" {KJV). God will make provision for us, and the Lord is always on time. The storm can't win, God has your destiny in his hands.

It is essential to let the Lord fight the battle for you and stand back before it gets too far out of control. When we will get in the right position with God, and it is imperative not to move to the left or the right just stand still in that place. When your life feels so overwhelmed, and out of control it is time to let it go, and God able handle it for you.

There are many issues in life you can't manage on your own, example it is like trying to climb a mountain, and it is too high to reach. There is no river too wide or valley too deep that God can't deliver you. "All power is given unto me in heaven and in earth" (KJV). God already knew us before created you, and some things in life out of your control only God can move the obstacles out of the way. The Lord is greater than any problem in our life, and no one can monopolize God's plan. God able to protect you from any storm that tries to rise against you. The storm can't win, God has your destiny in his hands.

"He brought me up also out of the horrible pit, out of the miry clay, and set my feet upon a rock, and established my goings" KJV). There are some things we face in life; it seems you can't manage the problem, and God will put his divine protection up around us in the midst the storm. Do you understand why we need to be protected by God?

The Lord loves us, and we are unique God wants to protect his children. When you allow God to come in your life, and take care of you, and the Lord able to keep you allow nothing to penetrate through the blood of Jesus.

"We are trouble on every side, yet not distressed, we are perplexed, but not despair; persecuted, but not forsaken; cast down, but not destroyed" (KJV). The enemy will try to make you give up on God and want to make you miss out what God has for you. The storm can't win, God has your destiny in his hand.

We must keep praying and trusting God to help us to get in that place to serve him for his Glory. It is imperative we get in the right place God wants us to stay in his will. It was essential for you to continue to pray unto the Lord with a sincere heart, and the right Spirit.

when the storm is trying to hold you back, and trouble is on every side of you need to keep the faith. God will reach down to cover us in his arms and keep you from the hands of the enemy. "He that dwelleth in the secret place of the most High shall abide under shadow of the Almight" (KJV). I am now in that placed called "there" God is your keeper and provider for our life. You are now resting in the arms of God protecting you every day of your life. You are now walking into your destiny, and never look back. It is imperative to remember it does not matter how large or small the turmoil appears in your life the storm can't win, God has your destiny in his hands.